Produced by Copyright S.A.R.L., Paris, France
Editor: Jean-Nöel Mouret
Photography Matthieu Prier
Design: Christine Comte

Translated from the French by Charles Polley,
in association with First Edition Translations, Cambridge

3494
This 1995 edition published by Bramley Books
© 1995 this English-language edition
Bramley Books, Godalming, Surrey
All rights reserved
ISBN 1-85833-508-6
Printed and bound in Spain by Graficas Estella

KNIVES
OF THE WORLD

Jean-Noël Mouret

Bramley Books

AYANT EU UN JOUR L'HONNEUR D'ÊTRE INVITÉ À UNE BELLE TABLÉE EN COMPAG
D'UN GRAND PHOTOGRAPHE, D'UN INGÉNIEUR DU SON RENOMMÉ ET D'UN EXCELLE
ÉCRIVAIN, JE ME RAPPELLE L'INSTANT OÙ, LES PREMIERS PLATS ARRIVANT, NO
AVONS SORTI TOUS QUATRE UN LAGUIOLE DE NOTRE POCHE POUR FAIRE TINTER S
LA NAPPE LA LUMIÈRE DE NOS LAMES. NOUS N'AURIONS PAS ÉTÉ PLUS AGRÉAB
MENT SURPRIS EN DÉCOUVRANT QUE NOUS ÉMARGIONS AU MÊME SERVICE SECR
NOTRE CODE DE RALLIEMENT ÉTAIT L'ÉLÉGANTE MENACE DE LA LAME CAMBRÉ
L'ESPAGNOLE, LE FUSEAU BOMBÉ DU MANCHE QUI FLATTE LA MAIN, ENFIN LA BEL
DU RESSORT QUI PONCTUE L'ALLIANCE DE LA CORNE ET DE L'ACIER. COMME TOUS L
COUTEAUX DE LAGUIOLE FABRIQUÉS AUJOURD'HUI, CELUI QU'ABRITE CET ÉCRIN DE
CEND EN DROIT FIL DES PREMIERS MODÈLES ASSEMBLÉS EN 1829. MAIS, OUTRE QU
EST LE SEUL AUJOURD'HUI À ÊTRE RÉALISÉ À LAGUIOLE, IL A SA PROPRE HISTOIRE.
EST NÉ DE LA RENCONTRE ENTRE MES AMIS PHILIPPE STARCK ET JEAN LOUIS COST

LE PREMIER PRODIGUAIT À SON LAGUIOLE PERSONNEL LES SOINS ATTENTIFS QU'U
HONNÊTE MOUSQUETAIRE ACCORDE À SA RAPIÈRE. LE SECOND, ASSOCIÉ À U
GROUPE DE JEUNES ENTREPRENEURS DE L'AUBRAC, LUI PROPOSA D'EN ÉPURER L
LIGNE AFIN D'EN CONFIRMER LA MODERNITÉ D'ORIGINE ET DE CONCEVOIR UNE MAN
FACTURE OÙ LE FABRIQUER. CETTE MANUFACTURE, REPÉRABLE DE LOIN À LA GRAND
LAME POINTÉE VERS LE CIEL QUI DOMINE SES TOITS, FABRIQUE AUJOURD'HUI U
LAGUIOLE NUMÉROTÉ ADAPTÉ À LA CIVILISATION URBAINE. IL A POUR ÂME UNE LAM
EN ACIER CHIRURGICAL 440 RÉAIGUISABLE À L'INFINI ET POUR CORPS UN MANCHE E
ALUMINIUM MASSIF. L'ENTRETIEN EST SIMPLE : IL FAUT L'ESSUYER AVEC UNE MIE DE PA
PUIS AVEC SA SERVIETTE. IL FAUT LE REFERMER VERS SOI EN TENANT LE MANCH
D'UNE MAIN, LA LAME DE L'AUTRE. IL FAUT L'ÉCRIRE LAGUIOLE ET LE PRONONC
"LAÏOLE". IL FAUT DEMANDER UN SOU À CELUI OU À CELLE À QUI ON L'OFFRE POU
NE PAS COUPER L'AMITIÉ. UN LAGUIOLE EST UN COUTEAU DE PAIX. B. CHAPU

This knife is shown smaller than actual size.

CONTENTS

All knives illustrated in this book between pages 26 and 123 are shown actual size unless otherwise stated.

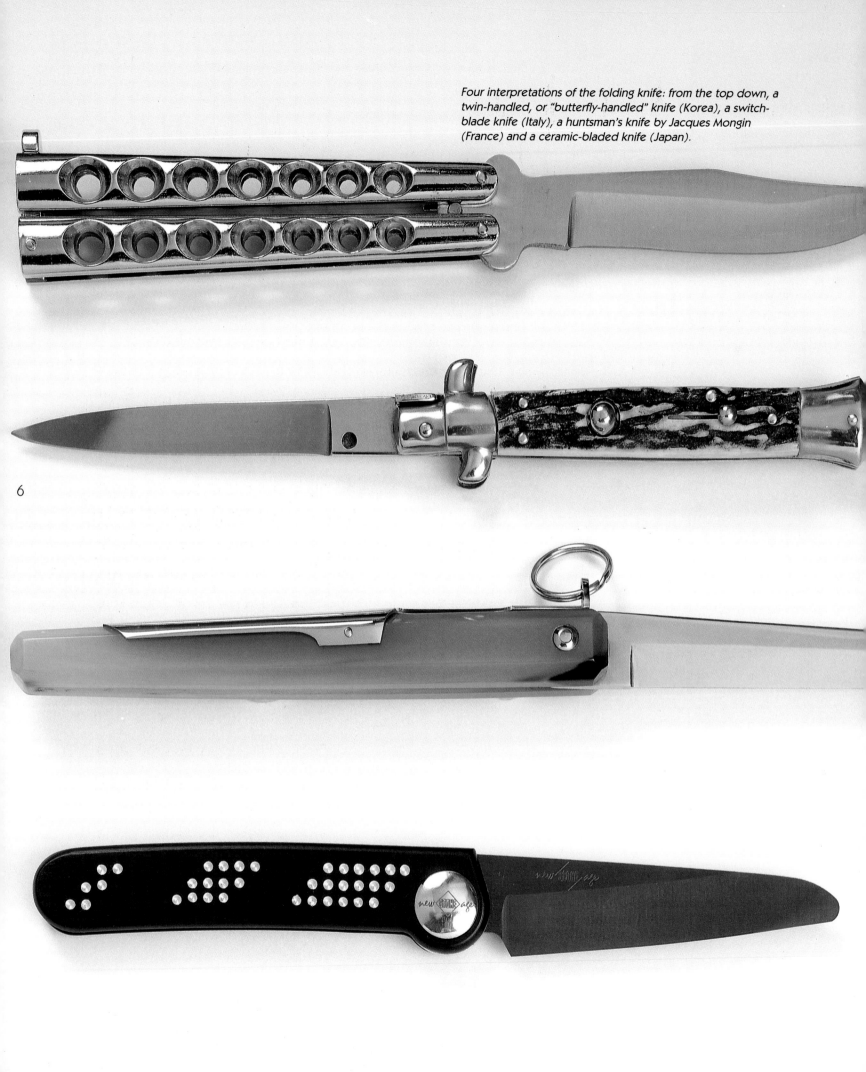

Four interpretations of the folding knife: from the top down, a twin-handled, or "butterfly-handled" knife (Korea), a switch-blade knife (Italy), a huntsman's knife by Jacques Mongin (France) and a ceramic-bladed knife (Japan).

6

Man's Best Friend

Man's oldest and most faithful companion is not the dog, but the knife.

Like all our forebears in every civilization down the ages, we use knives day in, day out, with hardly a second thought.

Yet when we actually think about it, the knife is the one thing we have inherited from our prehistoric ancestors that is still in everyday use. Ever since that day, long ago, when a man – who may not even have had the gift of fire at the time – first thought of extending his flint blade by attaching a wooden or bone handle to it, the knife has been an essential multi-purpose tool for preparing food, eating, cutting a stick, sharpening a pencil, stripping a wire, and so on, and even, but only in the last and most extreme resort, defending ourselves. And we are talking here about the simplest of knives, not the Swiss Officer's knife that is the nearest thing to a portable workshop!

It is amazing enough that an object so simple as a knife still has so much left to give after its long journey down the ages, yet we find new uses for it almost daily – our ancestors could never have conceived of repairing electrical wiring! What is even more fascinating is to discover the unending and imaginative variations on the theme of a blade and a handle. A rich variety of shapes, sizes, materials, opening systems and the like – this is what master cutlers have delighted in creating over the course of time.

7

These knives are shown larger than actual size.

8

From the Stone Age to the Modern Stone Age: flint blades (top).
Reproduction prehistoric knife (center) made by craftsman cutler M.
Ginelli (France) using the same materials as our early forebears:
chipped flint blade, wooden haft, boar gut binding. Bottom: knife
with a blade fashioned of fine ceramic (zirconium oxide).

ONE HUNDRED THOUSAND YEARS OF KNIVES

In September 1991, while negotiating the Similauy Glacier on the border between Austria and Italy, a party of Alpine walkers found a cadaver lying in a hollow of ice and water. For once, the glacier had not given up the body of a lost climber, but one of our New Stone Age forebears. He had

been dead more than 5,320 years, yet he and all the things he had with him were perfectly preserved. Among these was a superb flint knife complete with haft. This was no ceremonial knife intended for a nobleman or high priest, but one of the sturdy, everyday kind that must have existed by the thousand at that time, in a style that by then had probably been traditional for tens of thousands of years. It is the only one and the oldest of its kind to have survived intact. Though he

lived in the Bronze Age, this man still preferred the stone blade, for the simple reason that bronze is too soft to take a good enough cutting edge. Not until the discovery of iron would there be what we call today a "technological breakthrough," giving the knife its now familiar form and materials.

We know from the results of archeological investigations at sites such as Herculaneum and Pompeii that the knives used by the Romans and Greeks were very little different from

Above: chipped flint knife and polished stone ax from the "Hauslabjoch Man" (New Stone Age) (top). The obsidian blade (lower picture) is a reproduction prehistoric knife blade by Sillevold (Norway).

These knives are shown larger than life size.

So-called "scalping" knife (USA). The steel blade is hammered to suggest chipped flint. Ivory haft, leather.

Giant "Douk-Douk" folding knife.

Three knives based on a traditional Corsican design, crafted by Antonini of Bastia (France).

those we use today. The folding knife had already appeared; and as a supreme refinement, fruit knives had ivory or bone blades to avoid making the food taste of metal oxide.

As for scabbards and sheaths, the Celts had these in use well before the time of Christ.

Until the end of the 16th century the knife served the purpose of both knife and fork. It was used to cut and skewer a morsel of food and then lift it to the mouth. The knife did not assume its specialized role until later.

The 15th century saw the first appearance of knives with multiple blades and a number of instruments such as a spike, file or scissors.

At about the same time, when people usually brought their own knives to the meal-table, but found that knives with fixed blades were cumbersome, the folding knife was invented. The modern pocket knife had arrived. But not until 1880 was it commonly fitted with a corkscrew, which also was invented in the 18th century.

Meanwhile, the cutlery industry in its fullest sense had been developing under the influence of the Crusades. The most advanced techniques for forging and hardening steel known to the Orient were at once taken up in France, where the best-known centers for cutlery were Thiers, Châtellerault, Toulouse, Langres, Nogent, Nevers, Cosne-sur-Loire, Caen, Tinchebray (near Rouen), Saint-Etienne and Périgueux (where the Nontron knife is probably a continuation of the same tradition). Many of these centers disappeared during the French Revolution, but some, such as Thiers and Nogent, are still operating.

Cutlery and knives made more progress in a single century than in all the thousands of years that went before. Sadly, many regional types of knives intended for customers living in the country ceased production as rural populations declined. Such was the case with the Rouen knife, manufactured locally until about 1870 and then at Thiers until 1960. Many other country designs are currently under threat – collectors please note!

By contrast, basic materials underwent a rapid phase of modernization: 440 steel (surgical stainless steel) was widely introduced, replacing carbon steel which was too liable to rust. Dishwasher-proof handles appeared on the scene. But the main and most noticeable innovation was in fine ceramics. A spin-off from space research, this new material is based on metal oxides, and is extremely sharp and wear-resistant. Progress, then, seems to be taking us into another stone age!

Alongside industrial production, there are increasing numbers of craftsmen throughout the world, fashioning knives that are often unique in their originality. This revival of high artistry in knife creation is a growing trend.

Even after hundreds of thousands of years, the history of the knife is still being written.

Three knives from the new generation of fine ceramics, with steel blades coated in diamond-carbon: two kitchen knives and a foie gras knife (courtesy GTI).

11

A knife from the manufacturer Laguiole as conceived by designer Yann Pennors. The handle is made of carbon-fiber.

Diamond-carbon bladed carving set in a presentation case decorated with a synthetic zirconium oxide stone (courtesy GTI).

YANIP INOX

E.DEHILLERIN

18r.Coquilliere

30

THE CUTLER'S ART

The quality and value of a knife therefore depend on the combination of all these aspects: the quality of the chosen materials, the care that goes into forging the blade, the quality of machining and assembly.

We can now examine the main stages in manufacturing a traditional Laguiole knife, as carried out in the workshops of master cutlers "Le couteau de Laguiole" ("Laguiole Knives").

The basic materials are these: 440 C steel (sharpenable martensitic stainless steel, known as surgical steel) for the blade; brass for the handle linings (or scales) and the bolsters (reinforcements at the ends of the handles); and horn or rosewood for the handle coverings.

The bars of 440 C steel are cut into sections or "strings." The strings are heated to 1,100°C (more than 2,000°F) and then forged on the 300-tonne drop hammer. After that they are re-heated in an electric furnace and hardened by quenching in an oil bath. The rough forged blades are then heated once more, but to a rather lower temperature, and quenched again: this is known as tempering.

Above: from the rough forged blade to the finished "smithed" blade (top). The drop hammer (lower picture).

These knives are shown larger than actual size.

Hardening steel in a mineral oil bath.

Rough forgings brought to red heat.

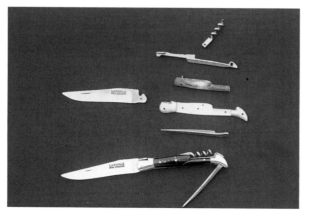

The various components of a Laguiole knife.

The cutting edge is formed by grinding, also called honing or sharpening.

Positioning the rivet hole in a blade is critical. If it is off center, the blade will pivot incorrectly and jam the opening mechanism.

Meanwhile the springs are cut and machined from sheet steel, while linings and bolsters are cut and formed.

Handle coverings and implements (corkscrew, spike, etc.) are handled separately, as is the distinctive bee motif traditionally placed above the joint on Laguiole knives.

In all, there will be several dozen parts on the bench by the time the assembler comes to rivet them together entirely by hand.

The simplest knives are those with fixed blades. Folding knives are always jointed where the blade and handle meet, and this joint must be made with great care. Most "folders" have a device for locking the blade. This may be manual, such as a twist-ring (e.g. Nontron, Opinel), or a haft-lock that may be external (as with the butterfly-handled knife) or internal (as in the case of the Colt system). On the other hand it may be automatically operated by a spring inside the handle (e.g. Laguiole, pump-action mechanisms, the "liner lock" system, etc.) or by external means such as the Navaja release-ring joint.

The greater the number of accessories such knives carry (spike, corkscrew, saw, etc.), the more complex it becomes to assemble them, since each must be able to pivot and needs a spring to hold it closed or open.

Following assembly and inspection, the whole knife is polished and the blade is given its final sharpening on a diamond grinding-wheel.

The manufacturing process is exactly the same for the "new" designer Laguioles such as the Philippe Stark model with aluminum handle coverings, and the design by Yann Pennor's with carbon fiber coverings (and Damascus blade in some versions).

As a result of all this care, present-day Laguiole knives can withstand the ravages of time and are handed down, like their 19th-century predecessors, from generation to generation.

Clearly a high-quality knife that can last a lifetime, with minimum maintenance and a good, easily sharpened cutting edge, is not going to be cheap, though in general the price will be very affordable. Better to "invest" in a reputable brand than a low-priced copy that will soon disappoint.

If you want to know more about cutlery, the Maison des Couteliers in Thiers (Puy-de-Dôme), France, arranges tours of its workshops. If you are tempted to try your hand at making a knife, you can very easily get the basic materials from some cutlers and gunsmiths, and even take a course with a master craftsman. You can find out what is available by visiting cutlery shows and exhibitions, or by reading specialist magazines such as *Blade and Knife* (both published in the USA).

Positioning the blade rivet.

Assembling a knife by hand.

15

Final sharpening.

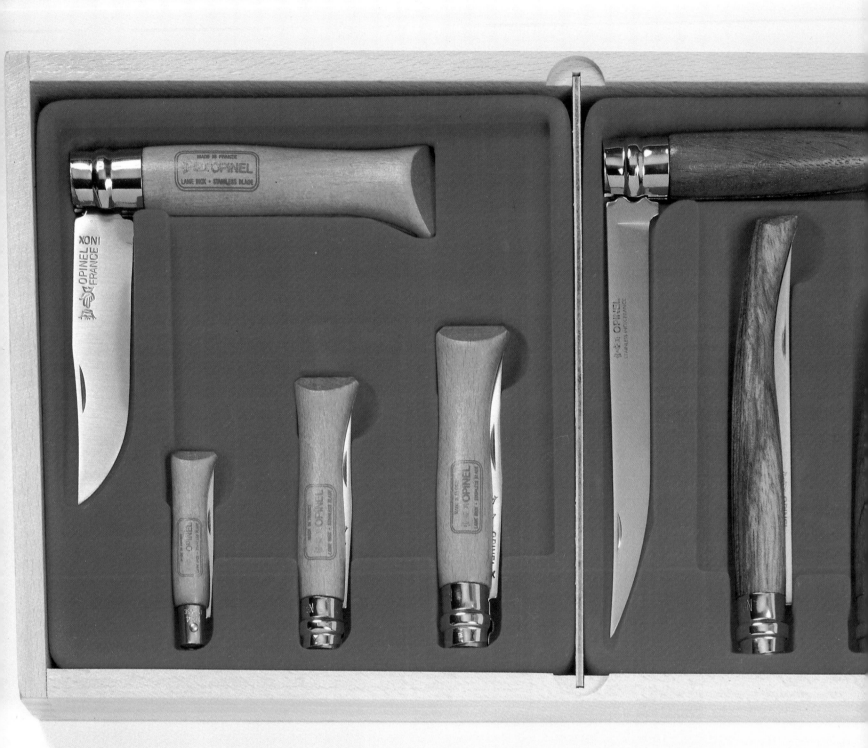

Opinel, France's best-known and most popular range of pocket
knives: left, the traditional model; right, the new range featuring the
"fish fillet" blade.

POCKET KNIVES

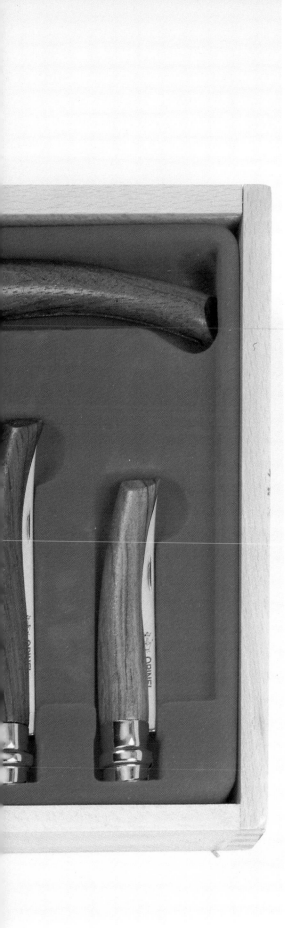

Cutting a stick from a hedge, trimming an animal's hoof, opening a bottle of wine, cutting meat, slicing a mushroom – the thousand and one traditional uses for the pocket knife reflect its rural origins. It started with the farm-worker and the shepherd, who needed something simple and sturdy made of local materials, like carbon steel (in 19th-century France the countryside was dotted with little blast-furnaces and forges), and for the handles, local wood like beech or box, or horn from their sheep and cattle. Nearly all were folding knives, to make them easier to carry. There is an immense variety, from the simple, single-bladed folding knife with no locking device, to the multiple instrument with six or even eight implements, coming close to the Swiss Officer's knife.

Many of these knives had, and in fact still have, an instrument for the hunter called a cartridge extractor. It sometimes takes the form of a pair of hooks at the head of the haft that also acts as a guard, but may be a serrated, folding accessory. In the days when cartridges were made of cardboard, this handy little gadget made light work of extracting any that had swollen with the damp.

Blade-locking systems, where fitted, also take many forms: the twist-ring (e.g. Nontron, Opinel), the mild spring (Laguiole), the spring-loaded release button, the spring-loaded external pull-and-release ring, and so on.

Right now the "home-grown" pocket knife is undergoing a new surge of interest that seems set to continue. And so it should!

17

These knives are shown smaller than actual size.

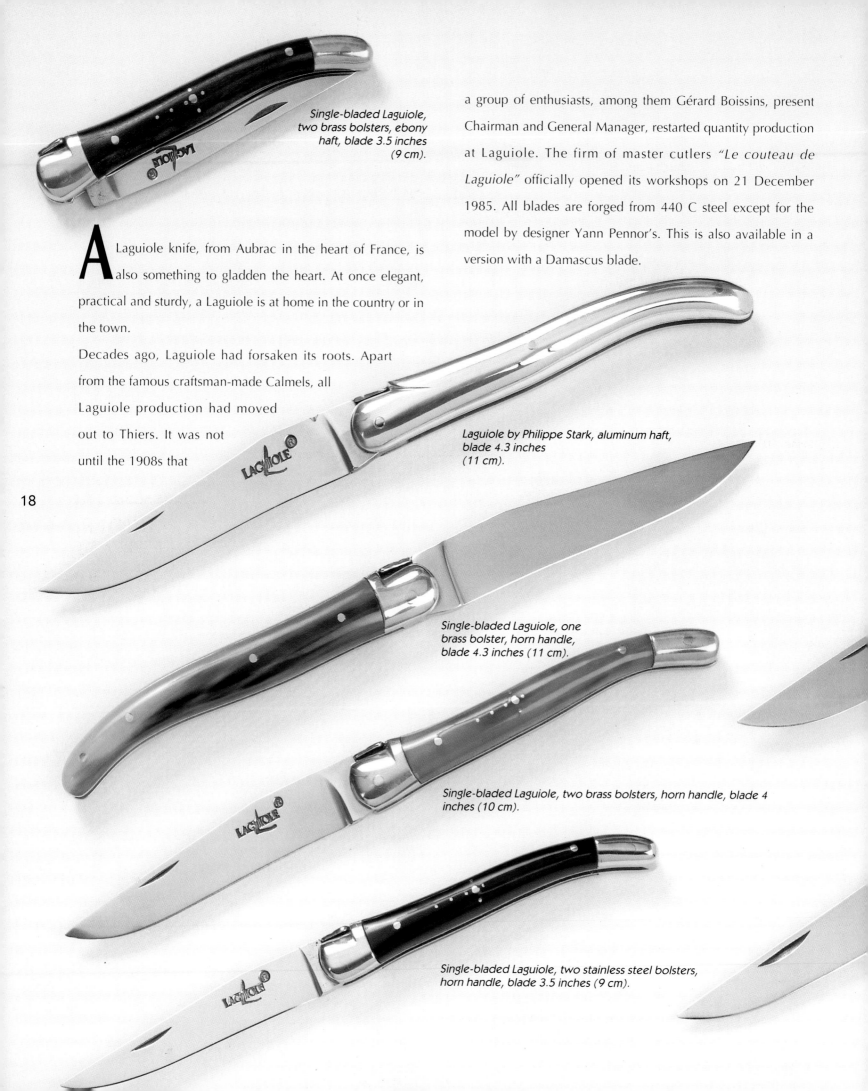

Single-bladed Laguiole, two brass bolsters, ebony haft, blade 3.5 inches (9 cm).

A Laguiole knife, from Aubrac in the heart of France, is also something to gladden the heart. At once elegant, practical and sturdy, a Laguiole is at home in the country or in the town.

Decades ago, Laguiole had forsaken its roots. Apart from the famous craftsman-made Calmels, all Laguiole production had moved out to Thiers. It was not until the 1908s that a group of enthusiasts, among them Gérard Boissins, present Chairman and General Manager, restarted quantity production at Laguiole. The firm of master cutlers *"Le couteau de Laguiole"* officially opened its workshops on 21 December 1985. All blades are forged from 440 C steel except for the model by designer Yann Pennor's. This is also available in a version with a Damascus blade.

18

Laguiole by Philippe Stark, aluminum haft, blade 4.3 inches (11 cm).

Single-bladed Laguiole, one brass bolster, horn handle, blade 4.3 inches (11 cm).

Single-bladed Laguiole, two brass bolsters, horn handle, blade 4 inches (10 cm).

Single-bladed Laguiole, two stainless steel bolsters, horn handle, blade 3.5 inches (9 cm).

Two-piece Laguiole (blade and spike), two brass bolsters, azobe haft, blade 4.3 inches (11 cm).

Three-piece Laguiole, no bolsters, horn handle, blade 4.7 inches (12 cm).

LAGUIOLE, THE HEART OF FRANCE

Two-piece Laguiole (blade and corkscrew), two brass bolsters, horn handle, blade 4.3 inches (11 cm).

Single-bladed Laguiole, no bolsters, horn handle, blade 4.7 inches (12 cm).

In 1890, when Joseph Opinel from Savoie first developed the folding knife that would carry his name, did he ever imagine that he was creating something that would be an influence in the 20th century, to the extent that Opinel has become synonymous with "Made in France" as far afield as the United States?

Simple, practical, well-balanced and built to last, the Opinel has continued almost unchanged, except for the recent introduction of stainless steel blades. All Opinel knives are folding, and use the same twist-ring blade locking system as the Nontron knife.

This twist-ring, with the patented name "Virobloc," incorporates a circular enlargement that acts as a guide when it rotates around the head of the pivot. It is not perfectly cylindrical, but slightly offset on the side toward the blade, ensuring a perfect lock even if the pivot develops a certain amount of play in the course of use. A genuine Opinel is distinguished by the "crowned hand" mark stamped or imprinted on the blade. "Basic" versions have a varnished beech-wood handle featuring a rectangular stamp with the words *"Opinel, La Main Couronnée"* ("Opinel, The Crowned Hand"). A black stamp means the blade is carbon steel and red means it is stainless.

Three de luxe Opinel knives assembled by Mongin exclusively for the firm of Courty et Fils. The handles are, from the top down, micarta, buffalo and pale horn respectively.

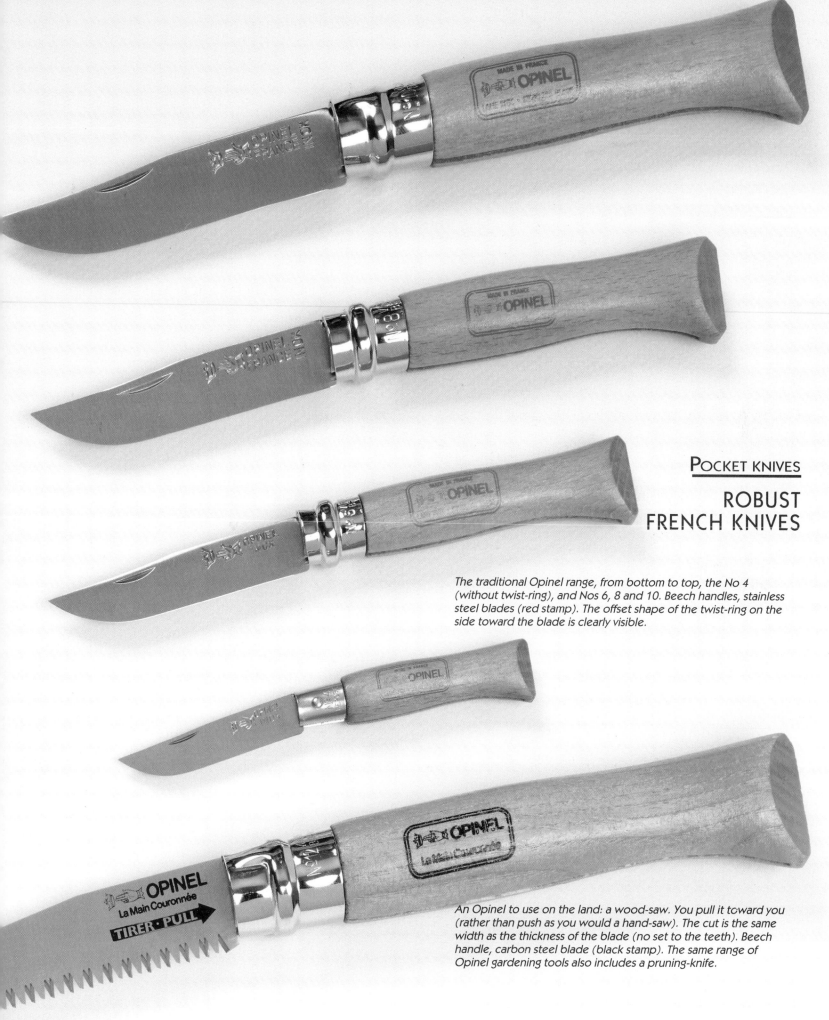

ROBUST FRENCH KNIVES

The traditional Opinel range, from bottom to top, the No 4 (without twist-ring), and Nos 6, 8 and 10. Beech handles, stainless steel blades (red stamp). The offset shape of the twist-ring on the side toward the blade is clearly visible.

An Opinel to use on the land: a wood-saw. You pull it toward you (rather than push as you would a hand-saw). The cut is the same width as the thickness of the blade (no set to the teeth). Beech handle, carbon steel blade (black stamp). The same range of Opinel gardening tools also includes a pruning-knife.

22

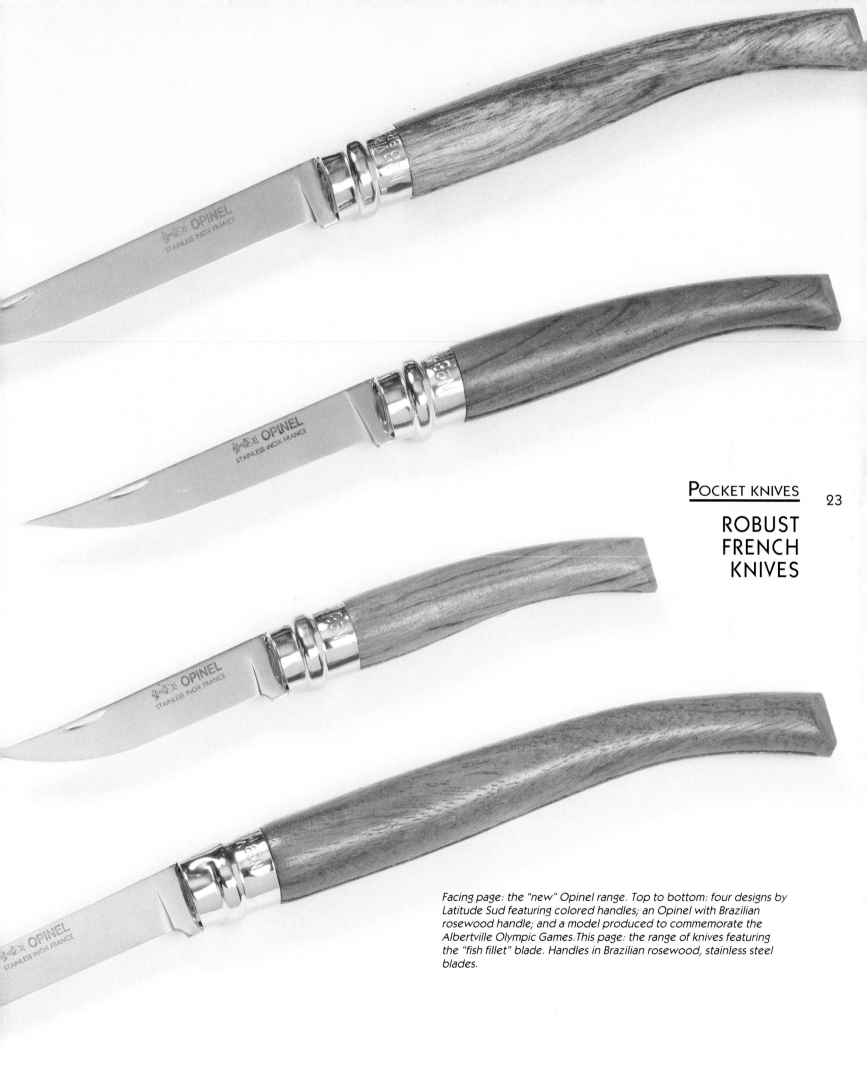

ROBUST
FRENCH
KNIVES

Facing page: the "new" Opinel range. Top to bottom: four designs by Latitude Sud featuring colored handles; an Opinel with Brazilian rosewood handle; and a model produced to commemorate the Albertville Olympic Games. This page: the range of knives featuring the "fish fillet" blade. Handles in Brazilian rosewood, stainless steel blades.

Many of these faithful servants are still in production today, so we shall take a look at some of them now before they are all snapped up at market stalls.

Knives for the country-dweller, lying forgotten in some sideboard or farm-table drawer, gently gather rust till next time they are used, and then just a quick sharpening gives them a whole new lease of life. There are literally thousands of these traditional knives, serving generation after generation, not usually expensive, always with carbon-steel blades and therefore liable to tarnish, but always ready to take a keen edge.

24

A very popular model by Coursolle of Thiers: carbon-steel blade, corkscrew, copper handle coverings impressed with a variety of motifs. The key-ring on the left is from the same maker.

Rustic knife known as an "Alpine." This is a simple folding knife with no blade lock. Made by Pradel.

Traditional four-piece knife. The guard is also a cartridge extractor. Deer horn handle.

Rustic knife known as a "Capuchin." This is a simple folding knife with a Brazilian rosewood haft and carbon-steel blade. Made by Arbalète.

Rustic knife known as a "barrel." Another simple folder with a carbon-steel blade, by Pradel.

ROBUST FRENCH KNIVES

Vendetta: this design, with more than a hint of folklore to it, has been influenced by the traditional knife of Corsica.

Three-piece knife from Alsace. The small blade and corkscrew remind us that the region has a long tradition of wine-making! Made by G. David.

A different handle illustration for this two-piece from Coursolle: the scouting motif tells us the customer they have in mind!

Eight-piece Isarinox knife, clearly influenced by the Swiss style. All stainless steel.

Two de luxe interpretations of the two-piece pocket knife: ivory coverings (left); tortoise-shell (right). Stainless steel blades. Made exclusively for Courty et Fils.

The same model as the four-piece knife on page 24, shown here closed: the guard hooks acting as cartridge extractors and the blade-release catch are clearly visible.

Traditional six-piece knife with pale horn handle. Made by Mongin for Courty et Fils.

ROBUST FRENCH KNIVES

Folding knife in the Boussadia design from the "Bundu" range, originally made for export to Lebanon. Carbon-steel blade, rounded handle coverings of thin stamped sheet metal with simulated bolsters. The blade lock is in fact purely for decoration.

ideal for making hard-wearing handles.

The Nontron knife gradually evolved, but it held firm to its original materials, namely the forged steel "sage leaf" blade, copper twist-ring locks, and poker-work boxwood handle decorated with two rows of small dots and a horseshoe shape known as a *"mouche"* ("fly"). This unusual pyrography is said to be based on a Moorish design.

From the 15th century, cutlers from Paris used to stay over in Nontron, a large township in the Dordogne, in order to learn the secrets of the craft. Legend also tells us that Ravaillac, who assassinated the French king, Henri IV, was armed with a Nontron. All this gives us some idea of the age and quality of the cutlery tradition in Nontron. The region was in fact ideally suited to this industry. Rich in iron ore, blessed with the clear waters of the river Bandiat for hardening and tempering the steel, it had an abundant supply of boxwood,

28

An intriguing mixture of traditional and modern, this "carp's tail" handle made of multi-colored inlaid laminated wood. An experiment that was taken no further.

Unlike their larger cousins, "little" Nontrons are fitted with a fixed locking-ring. They are folding knives all the same.

NONTRON KNIVES

Four fine examples of the Nontron knife. From top to bottom: classic knife handle fitted with a notched blade in the so-called "Catalan" style; a double twist-ring model; the "carp's tail" handle that made a brief appearance in the 19th century and is starting to make a comeback; and the ball-handled knife, typical of the 18th century and still being produced. These designs have a feature in common that would be remarkable even on a fixed-blade knife: the handle thickens toward the blade. This stops the hand sliding forward and gives an amazingly comfortable grip.

30

Douk-Douk knives were popular in all the former French colonies. They were very cheap, and produced in astronomical numbers – in those days they were sold by the gross. Despite that they were not in the least shoddy. To prove it, the colonies are no more than a memory, but the Douk-Douk is still very much with us.

THE DOUK-DOUK AND ITS COMPANIONS

The shape of the Douk-Douk blade has a vaguely Arabic look. These knives were originally intended for Melanesia, which accounts for the witch-doctor motif on the handle. Variants take the form of the El Baraka, produced for the Maghreb territories of northwest Africa; the Tiki, bound for Oceania and decorated with a Tahitian idol; and the Squirrel, made for the French market, with a blade shaped in what was called the "Bourbonnais" style.

They all have a sheet steel handle bent into a U enclosing a spring to hold the blade open or closed, a belt ring and a carbon-steel blade. Some current models have a stainless steel blade. These can be identified by the number "440" stamped near the joint.

The Spyderco knife (USA) with a blade by Seki (Japan). This highly contemporary folding knife is regarded as one of the best pocket knives of our time. There are many different sizes available, as well as various shapes of blade both with and without teeth.

Pump-action folding knife designed by Al Mar (USA). The Japanese blade is 440 C steel, the handle is stainless steel and Brazilian

32

"Elvis" folding knife. The American influence is obvious. Manufactured by Cartailler-Deluc (France): 440 steel blade, aluminum haft.

Pump-action folding knife in "Ranger's Knife" design by Poyet-Coursolle (France). Brazilian rosewood handle.

"Ranch" model folding knife by Éloi (France). It is opened by turning the wheel at the joint, and closed by pressing a catch. Micarta handle.

Pump-action folding knife by Herbertz (Germany). Blade 440 stainless steel, micarta handle.

Pump-action folding knife by Gerber (USA). Rubber handle.

AMERICAN INFLUENCE

Timberlite knife from Timberline (USA). Transparent plastic handle. The blade is released by pushing it forward.

Pump-action folding knife from Puma (Germany). Brazilian rosewood handle.

The classic of them all, the yardstick by which all other modern folding knives are measured: the pump-action Buck (USA), model 110 FG ("FG" stands for "fingers" because of the finger-recesses in the handle).

Knife with yataghan blade by Jacques Mongin (France). Stainless steel blade, pale horn handle.

All the knives shown here have the Navaja release-ring assembly: a strong, notched spring on the back of the haft engages with notches on the blade-tangs when opened, locking them in place. The ring is a pull-release. On multi-purpose knives, each implement (except the corkscrew) has a locking notch. The system is strong enough to survive the severest test.

French two-piece knife called a "huntsman." Stainless steel blades, deer horn handle.

Cornillon knife (France), four-piece. Stainless steel blades, deer horn handle.

UNTIRING
STRENGTH

"Moderne" knife by Jacques Mongin (France). Stainless steel blades, micarta handle.

Two-bladed "shuttle" knife from Jacques Mongin (France). Stainless steel blades, pale horn handle. This angle clearly shows the sizable spring on the back of the handle, its locking notches, the blade-tang notches and the release-ring.

Two classic little hunting knives: the Indiana knife (Italy) with a Colt opening system and a Buck knife in the Bucklock style (USA).

HUNTING

KNIVES

Hunting knives are handed down to us from the days when a hunter would never use anything else but cold steel. They are not the same as huntsman's knives, which are mostly meant for use with firearms, as is clear from the implements they carry, like cartridge extractors, choke screwdrivers and so on – as well as usually a corkscrew, for when the shooting party gets together for a bite to eat.

The functional and efficient hunting knife will have none of this. Depending on country of origin, we may find blades for use in hunting with horse and hounds, such as daggers and dirks for dispatching wounded quarry; blades for trappers – the so-called "skinners" knives, with wide, curving blades for removing animal pelts; or blades for dressing game.

Guns and hunting-rifles seem to have reduced the hunting knife to the status of an accessory in Western Europe, but it is still very much the custom in the United States, home of the legendary Bowie Knife that helped to win the West. This is said to owe its name to Colonel James Bowie, who fought to the death in 1836 at the Alamo armed with just such a knife.

Scandinavian cutlers have a special place in the history of hunting knives. Very decidedly knives of the outdoors, based on Lapp designs, their stocky blades are equally good for dressing game or gutting and cleaning large fish like trout or salmon. You do not have to live north of the Arctic Circle to appreciate that these are magnificent collector's items, especially as they are made entirely by hand within a thriving and continuous tradition of craftsmanship.

37

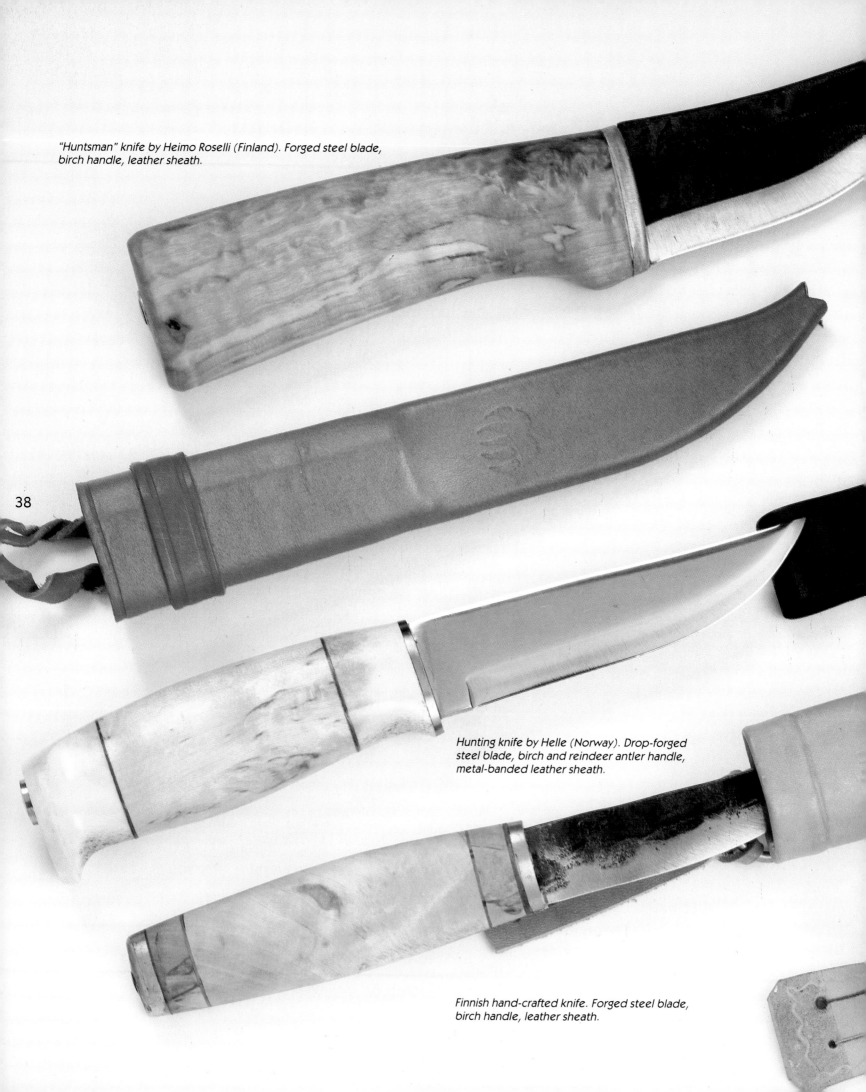

"Huntsman" knife by Heimo Roselli (Finland). Forged steel blade, birch handle, leather sheath.

Hunting knife by Helle (Norway). Drop-forged steel blade, birch and reindeer antler handle, metal-banded leather sheath.

Finnish hand-crafted knife. Forged steel blade, birch handle, leather sheath.

Fiskars knife (Finland): an interesting interpretation of the traditional Scandinavian knife adapted to quantity production.

FISKARS
STAINLESS FINLAND

TAPIO WIRKKALA

SCANDINAVIAN
CRAFTSMANSHIP

Craftsman-made knife from Finland. Its leather sheath is in colors and designs that are traditional among Lapplanders.

"Grandfather" knife by Heimo Roselli (Finland). Forged steel blade, birchwood haft, sheath of leather, birchwood and reindeer fur.

Knife from Helle (Norway). Drop-forged steel blade, birchwood handle, punched leather sheath.

Knife from Helle (Norway). Drop-forged steel blade, wooden handle, leather sheath.

SCANDINAVIAN CRAFTSMANSHIP

H. Roselli

HANDMADE IN FINLAND

Another style from Heimo Roselli (Finland).

42

These two knives from Helle (Norway) are a break with tradition. The blades are made of three-layer sandwich steel (a hard layer for the cutting edge sandwiched between two layers of a more flexible grade for strength). The upper knife has a walnut haft with solid brass guard and pommel. The handle of the lower one is made of banded leather with solid brass fittings. The sheaths are leather.

SCANDINAVIAN CRAFTSMANSHIP

Yisakki Järvenpää Oy
Stainless Finland

Angler's knife by Yisakki (Finland) with a long, fine blade for filleting fish. Drop-forged, stainless steel blade, birchwood handle, leather sheath with salmon motif.

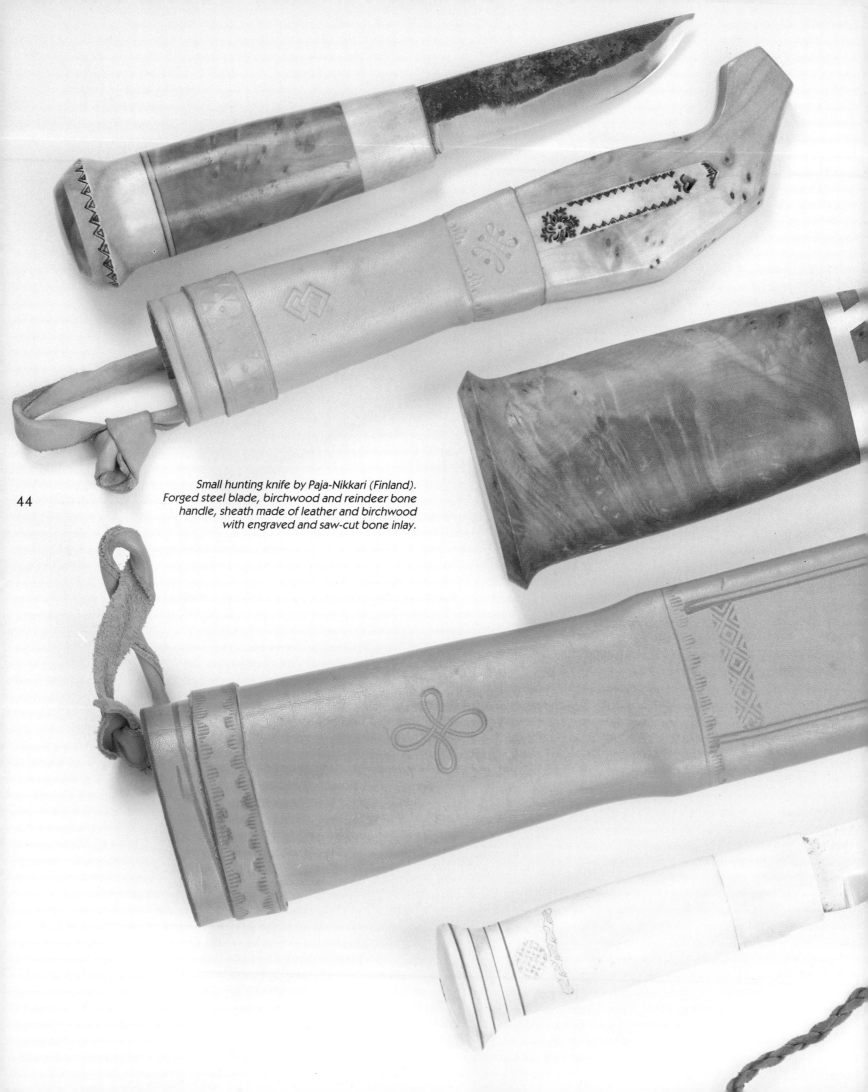

44

Small hunting knife by Paja-Nikkari (Finland). Forged steel blade, birchwood and reindeer bone handle, sheath made of leather and birchwood with engraved and saw-cut bone inlay.

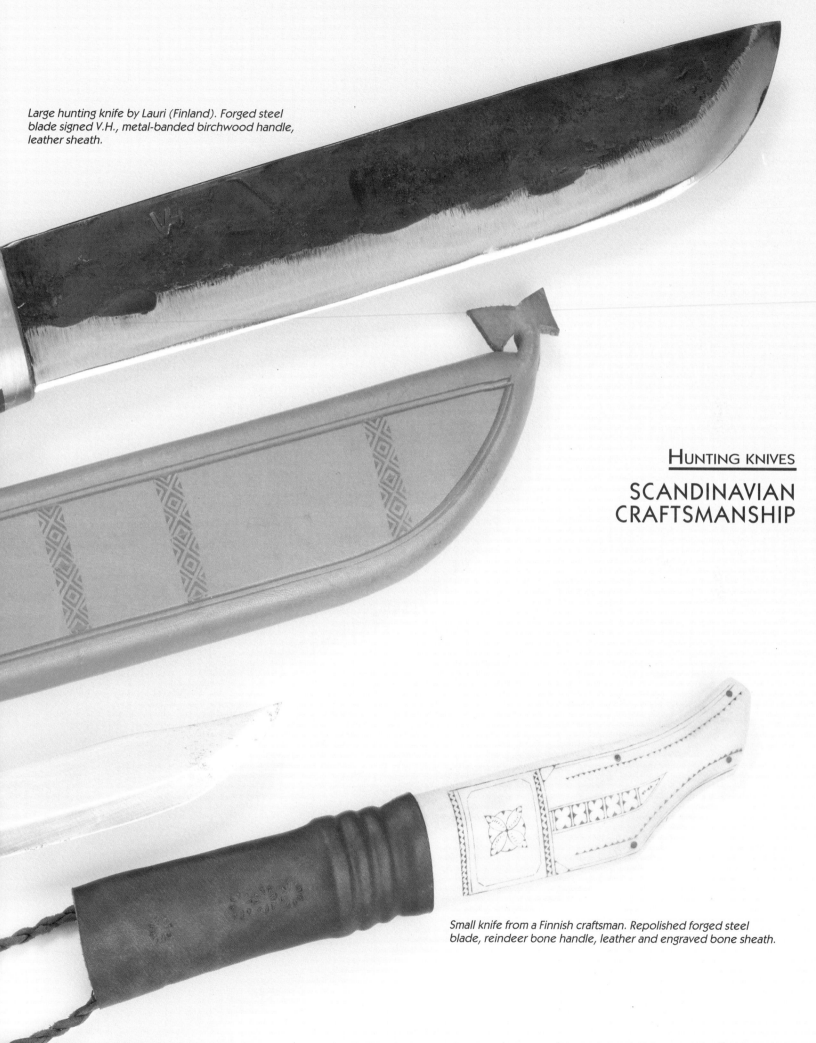

Large hunting knife by Lauri (Finland). Forged steel blade signed V.H., metal-banded birchwood handle, leather sheath.

SCANDINAVIAN CRAFTSMANSHIP

Small knife from a Finnish craftsman. Repolished forged steel blade, reindeer bone handle, leather and engraved bone sheath.

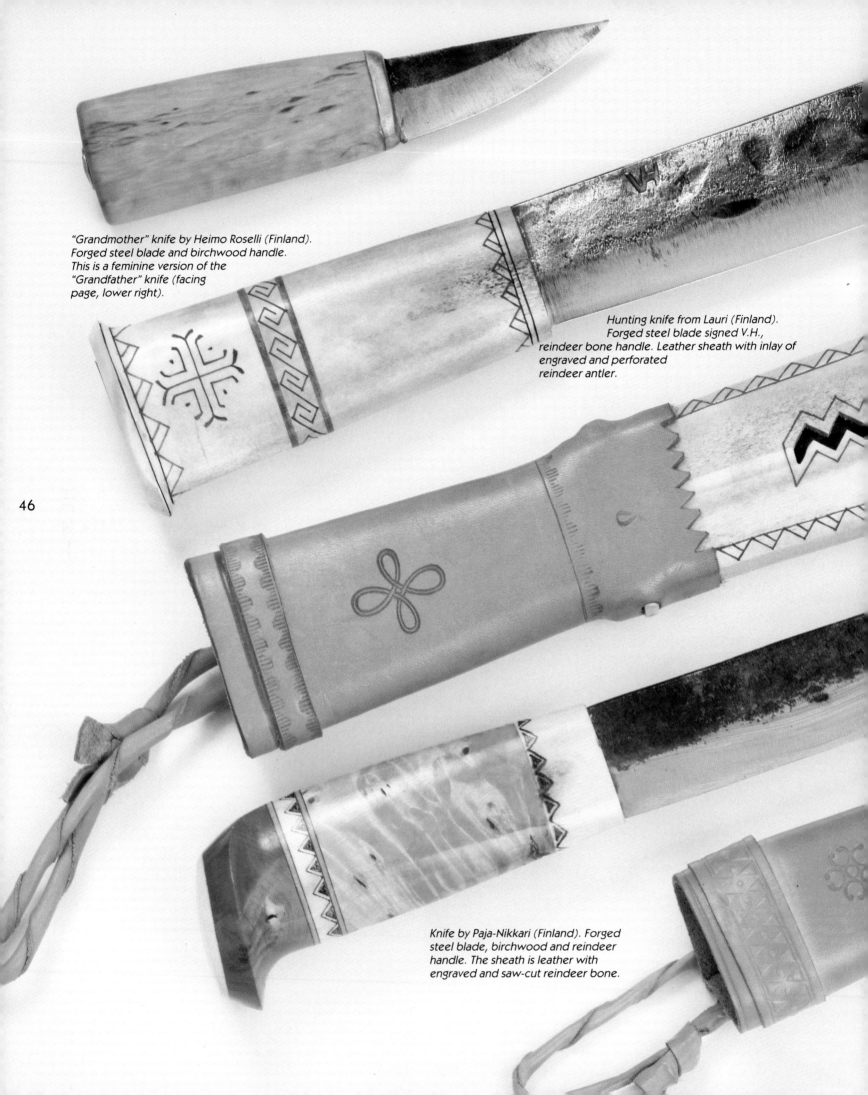

"Grandmother" knife by Heimo Roselli (Finland). Forged steel blade and birchwood handle. This is a feminine version of the "Grandfather" knife (facing page, lower right).

Hunting knife from Lauri (Finland). Forged steel blade signed V.H., reindeer bone handle. Leather sheath with inlay of engraved and perforated reindeer antler.

46

Knife by Paja-Nikkari (Finland). Forged steel blade, birchwood and reindeer handle. The sheath is leather with engraved and saw-cut reindeer bone.

SCANDINAVIAN CRAFTSMANSHIP

"Grandfather" knife by Heimo Roselli (Finland). Compare this knife to the one shown on page 40. These knives are entirely hand-made, and the differences are obvious at once. Each one is unique.

"Camargue" hunting knife, manufactured by the Maison des Couteliers in Thiers (France): 440 steel blade. Half-guard handle with ebony coverings on each side engraved with a horse's head. Sole-plate mounting (blade and tang plate solid-forged as a single piece).

"Adventure" knife from the Maison des Couteliers (France): 440 C steel blade, micarta handle coverings, sole-plate mounting.

48

"Prairie II" knife by Jean Tanazacq (France): 440 steel blade, leather and brass handle. Tang mounting (the blade has an extension in the form of a rod that fits into the handle).

Horseman's hunting dagger, manufactured by Éloi (France). Stainless steel blade, deer horn handle.

"Français IV" knife by Jean Tanazacq (France). Brass half-guard and pommel, Brazilian rosewood handle. Tang mounting.

50

Two trappers' knives manufactured by Grohmann (Canada). These are known as "skinners" knives and have a wide, curving blade to prevent damage to animal pelts. Stainless steel blade, Indian rosewood handle, brass rivets.

Two hunting daggers with folding blades, ideally suited for the hunt with horse and hounds. In the fully open position (above), it can be used as a hunting dagger. When closed (below), the blade can be used as a knife.

The pictures show, top, a Bogon dagger (France), stainless steel blade, deer-horn style handle, lever closure. At the foot of the page, a Hubertus dagger (Germany), stainless steel blade, deer horn handle, latch closure. Leather sheath.

BLADES FOR THE PROFESSIONAL HUNTER

"Double Shadow" dagger by Gil Hibben.

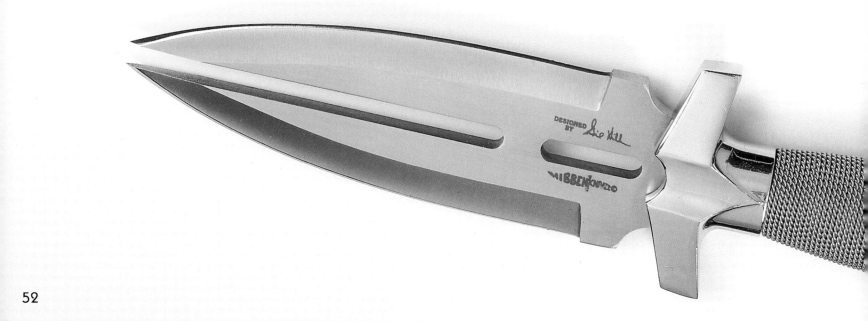

52

COMBAT KNIVES

The least pleasant aspect of the knife has to be faced: the deadly stealth of the cold steel weapon.

Most combat knives draw on the military for their inspiration. Designed and manufactured first and foremost for the armed forces, a civilian version becomes available only later.

Other than weapons collectors or those of a murderous disposition, what reason could anyone have for buying a combat knife? For one thing, they make excellent – perhaps the very best – sporting and outdoor knives. Designed for use under the most arduous conditions, they are strong enough to withstand even the severest test. Some are made of such high-grade steel that their blades can be used as can-openers without damaging the cutting edge! They are always assembled with the utmost care, and fit the hand beautifully. Not surprizingly, they command a high price, but are excellent value for money.

One of the best known creators of combat knives is the American, Alfred Clark Mar, also known as Al Mar. This veteran of the Green Berets, and former member of the US Special Forces, saw action in Laos and Thailand before setting up as a knife designer some ten or more years ago. His knives, as attractive as they are efficient, benefit from his war experience and are designed primarily for the US Army, the FBI and the CIA. Quite a customer list!

In the field of combat, throwing knives (and their Far Eastern counterpart, the "ninja" star) have a place of their own. Knife-throwing is to say the least a very exciting and highly-skilled sport.

53

This knife is shown larger than actual size.

Knife by G. Sakai (Japan). Combat design adapted to hunting and outdoor pursuits. Toothed blade in high-speed steel, micarta handle, rot-proof Cordura sheath (not shown).

54

"Gun Stock" knife by Al Mar, made in Japan, with a "semi-skinner" blade in 440 C steel. Half-guard. Pakka mahogany handle, set with the base of a genuine cartridge-case.

The all stainless steel "Silver Shadow" dagger designed by Gil Hibben. UC 441 steel blade, steel-wire wrapped handle, black leather sheath. Something of a collector's item, it blends the look of a parachute trooper's dagger with a hint of the Middle Ages.

THE "CIVILIAN" VERSIONS

"Government" combat knife by Sog (USA). The blade is made of extra-hard 57/58 RC stainless steel, the handle is roughened Kraton synthetic rubber and the sheath (not shown) is black leather.

Combat knife from Al Mar (USA) in the "Green Berets" series, designed for intensive military use, with 440 C steel blade, micarta handle. The bolster is engraved with the Latin motto De oppresso liber, meaning "Deliverance from tyranny."

Combat knife from Al Mar (USA), commemorating "Operation Desert Storm" (Gulf War). Limited edition, 440 C steel blade, brass guard, leather handle.

MIDDLE EAST WAR
16-JAN-1991
OPERATION *DESERT STORM*

Sog combat knife (USA). Extra-hard stainless steel blade, Kraton handle. This knife is in the same series as the one on the previous page.

FRANKLY MILITARY

Combat knife by Camilus (USA). This model is regulation US Army issue. Blade coated with anti-reflecting material, leather handle.

World War Two combat knife by Camilus (USA). Anti-reflecting blade, guard with thumb-rest, leather handle.

58

Ranger's combat knife. Black, double-edged, anti-reflecting blade, leather handle bound with brass wire, leather sheath (not shown).

"Special Air Service" commando knife. Double-edged blade bronzed for anti-reflecting effect, knurled brass handle, leather sheath with metal end-piece (not shown).

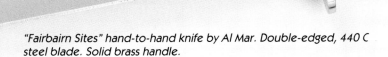

Short dagger in the "Equator" style by the Maison des Couteliers of Thiers (France). Double-edged, 440 C steel blade. Micarta handle with sole-plate mounting. Leather sheath. Subtler version of a rather "serious" hand-to-hand weapon.

KNIVES AND DAGGERS FOR CLOSE COMBAT

"Fairbairn Sites" hand-to-hand knife by Al Mar. Double-edged, 440 C steel blade. Solid brass handle.

Fighting knife of the British airborne commandos in the Second World War, later used by French parachute troops. Manufactured by Nowill & Sons of Sheffield (England). Handle and double-edged blade treated with anti-reflecting coat in one operation. Matt black leather sheath with metal end-piece (not shown). Authentic weapon of the period (private collection).

"Raid Gauloises" knife designed by Henri Viallon (France) and made by Aitor (Spain). Miniature saw on blade-back, micarta handle coverings. Sole-plate mounting. Leather sheath. Just made for the jungle!

KNIVES FOR THE SOLDIER OF FORTUNE

Military knife by Marto (Spain). Exact copy of the US Army regulation bayonet-knife. Miniature saw on blade-back, plastic handle. Sheath of nylon fabric and plastic reinforced with metal, multiple carrying points.

62

Its real name, balisong, reveals its Philippine origins. This is the knife of a country-dweller, sturdy, reliable and easy to manufacture with the minimum of special equipment. A discreet and daunting weapon.

Very popular at the present time, the double-handled, or "butterfly" knife owes its name to the characteristic handle, divided into two equal halves that fold over the blade when not in use and open out a full 180 degrees when needed.

WITH THE WINGS OF A BUTTERFLY

The examples shown here all have the Batangas mounting: the locking swivel is attached to the half-handle that faces the cutting edge when closed (unlike the Manila mounting, where the lock is attached to the half-handle that covers the back of the blade). Something worth knowing if you are attempting to open it with one hand!

Set of three solid-forged throwing knives in a triple sheath, made by Othello of Solingen (Germany). Below: solid-forged sports knife and a throwing star.

64

On this page, reading from the top down: "ninja" four-pointed star; brass-guarded throwing knife with cylindrical wood and metal handle; solid-forged throwing knife from Herbertz (Germany), designed for circus acts; and a small, solid-forged throwing knife.

THROWING WEAPONS

STEN
urfmesser

The ultimate expression of the multi-bladed knife and tool-set: multi-purpose cutter-pliers, a genuine pocket-size toolkit. Top: Toolclip from Sog (USA), made in Japan. Bottom: a design by Al Mar (USA) for the troops of the US Special Forces, also made in Japan. These are considered to be the most efficient knife-tools available at the present time.

66

KNIVES FOR THE HANDYMAN

When people began noticing the effects of technical progress on their everyday lives, the knife had to become more than just something used for cutting and stabbing. By the beginning of the 19th century, some pocket knives already included a corkscrew. Then the arrival of modern ammunition gave rise to the cartridge extractor. The invention of canned foods brought about the inclusion of the can-opener. Then came the screwdriver. New additions followed thick and fast, leading eventually to the twenty-nine or so accessories found on some Swiss knives, and even the hundred or more on a few craftsman-made masterpieces, though these more usually belong in museums.

There are now literally dozens of different kinds of gadget-knives available for specific purposes, trades or activities. Knives for the hunter, the angler, the diver, the camper, the sailing enthusiast, the electrician and so on. It has reached the point where it is hard to tell the difference between a multiple bladed pocket knife and a portable tool-kit. It is probably safe to say that any knife with one or more highly specialized accessories (compass, screwdriver, sophisticated cartridge extractor, etc.) is to all intents a gadget-knife or something very like it. In most cases, though, there is no room for doubt.

As we can see from the two gadget-knives shown here, designers are managing to incorporate ever-increasing numbers of accessories into ever-decreasing amounts of space, and their creativity is in full flood.

These knives are shown larger than actual size.

The Swiss Army knife came about in 1891 when the Swiss Army commissioned the association of master cutlers of Switzerland to manufacture a regulation pocket-knife locally, when previously it had been bought from Solingen (Germany).

This knife had to include a blade, a spike, a can-opener and a screwdriver. The contract was won by Charles Elsener, cutler at Ibach since 1884. In 1897 he patented a type known as the "Swiss Officer's Knife," that also had a small blade and a corkscrew. The Swiss Army knife was well and truly launched, soon to be followed by the brand-name Victorinox that Charles Elsener gave his firm in 1909 on the death of his mother, Victoria.

These days the market for the Swiss Army knife is shared between two rival brands, Victorinox and Wenger. The Swiss Army knife owes its success to its compact format, its lightness and its seemingly infinite versatility.

68

Good-quality copy of a Swiss knife, manufactured in France by Ducher of Thiers (shown open on next page).

Aluminum-handled "Military" Swiss knife by Wenger (shown open on next page).

Swiss knife by Wenger with 17 accessories. Some are multi-purpose, such as the graduated ruler and compass and the combined bottle-opener and screwdriver.

"SwissChamp" knife from Victorinox, complete with Swiss quartz watch and twenty-nine implements. Nine of these are standard: pocket blade (large), pen blade (small), corkscrew, can-opener and small screwdriver, bottle-opener and screwdriver with wire-stripper, reamer-spike. There are another twenty instruments: scissors, Phillips (cross-head) screwdriver, magnifying glass, angler's blade with scaler and magnetic disgorger including graduations in inches and centimetres, nail-file/metal-file, nail-cleaner with metal-saw, fine screwdriver, carrying-ring, tweezers, toothpick, wood-chisel, multi-purpose pliers with wire-cutter, mini-screwdriver (stored in the corkscrew), ball-pen.

Victorinox camping knife with twenty tools: the standard nine (see "SwissChamp" model above), plus scissors, wood-saw, wood-chisel, nail-file/metal-file, fine screwdriver, carrying-ring, tweezers, toothpick.

Victorinox driver's 10-piece knife
incorporating 17 gadgets.

"Military" knife by Wenger, 4 blades, 6 tools: blade, can-opener
with small screwdriver, spike, bottle-opener with screwdriver
(shown closed on previous page).

70

Copy of an 8-piece Swiss Army knife by Ducher (France). Large
blade, saw, can/bottle-opener, small blade, screwdriver with wire-
stripper, spike, corkscrew, gimlet (knife shown closed on previous
page).

"SwissChamp" knife from Victorinox in closed position. The watch is detachable. (Shown open on previous page).

Wenger 17-piece knife in closed position. The angle of this view shows how thick it is and explains why a belt-loop or case is so necessary! (Shown open on previous page).

The Victorinox camping knife in the closed position. A very compact 10-piece knife. (Shown open on previous page).

SWISS ARMY KNIVES

Standard Swiss knife from Victorinox, 6 accessories, 9 purposes. A direct descendant of the 1897 Swiss Officer's Knife. The model shown commemorates the Albertville Olympic Games.

Five-piece manicure knife by Victorinox: blade, nail-file, scissors, plus tweezers and toothpick.

Five-piece huntsman's knife by Beretta (Italy). Standard blade, curved game-dressing blade, saw, corkscrew and a special "rifle" blade. It has two notches numbered 12 and 20 on one side. These are cartridge extractors for each calibre. The two indentations on the other side (also numbered 12 and 20) are choke screwdrivers (for adjusting the tubes screwed to the end of the barrel to govern the spread of shot according to their length). It also has a built-in bottle-opener.

French multi-purpose 8-piece knife. Large blade, can/bottle-opener, scissors, screwdriver, small blade, spike, gimlet, corkscrew. Deer horn handle.

Military type, five-piece, multi-purpose Mauser knife complete with large blade, reamer-spike, corkscrew, special blade with Mauser markings and a wood-saw with double serrations (and a detachable blade-protector) together with a combined can/bottle-opener and screwdriver on the end.

NAME UNTER LIZENZ
DER MAUSER-WERKE
OBERNDORF GmbH.

MAUSER

KNIVES FOR THE
HANDYMAN

73

MULTI-
PURPOSE
MULTI-
BLADE

Rambler's knife made by Durol of Thiers (France). Button-release blade with built-in bottle-opener, spike, screwdriver, large carrying loop. Compass incorporated into the pommel. Ultra-light plastic handle.

Sailing enthusiast's four-piece knife: large blade, unshackler, screwdriver and spike. All stainless steel construction, nylon handle coverings, stainless steel and brass rivets.

Ready Edge multi-purpose cutter (USA).

74

Angler's knife with large switch-blade. Made by Hubertus of Solingen (Germany). The special tool, combining a fish-scaler, a bottle-opener and a stun-hammer, is opened by an automatic release-lever. Stainless steel blades, brass stun-hammer. Stainless steel, brass and Brazilian rosewood handle. Chain optional. This type of knife is more suitable for the freshwater angler. Some models are designed as weighing balances. In these the fish-scaler doubles as a graduated beam and the stun-hammer is the counterweight.

KNIVES FOR
THE ANGLER
AND THE
SAILING
ENTHUSIAST

*Two-piece sailing knife by Hubertus of Solingen (Germany). Large
blade and lever-released unshackler/spike. Stainless steel blades,
nylon handle, brass mountings.*

Ready Edge multi-purpose cutter (USA). Stainless steel serrated blade, plastic handle and sheath with key-ring attached. (Shown closed on previous page).

Combined knife and pliers from Leatherman (USA). Models shown are "Tool" (above) and "Mini-Tool" (right). Both of these folding tool-kits have a handle in two sections that folds over the pliers when not in use, similar to butterfly-handled knives (see p. 62). The "Tool" has twelve accessories including pliers, wire-cutters, large blade, file, can-opener, bottle-opener, screwdriver, graduated ruler (on the handle), spike etc. All stainless steel.

Folding combination knife and fork, described as "for the disabled." Designed to allow food to be cut and lifted with one hand. Stainless steel blade.

Outdoor cutter designed by Blackie Collins (USA). Stainless steel blade, plastic handle and sheath. Can be opened with one hand by pressing the release-button on the sheath.

Folding razor-knife by Bear MGC (USA): 440 steel blade, wooden handle.

Folding pocket knife styled like a tanto (Japanese-influenced blade shape) with switch-blade mechanism, made by Executive Edge (USA). When closed it can be carried in the pocket like a pen, which it resembles.

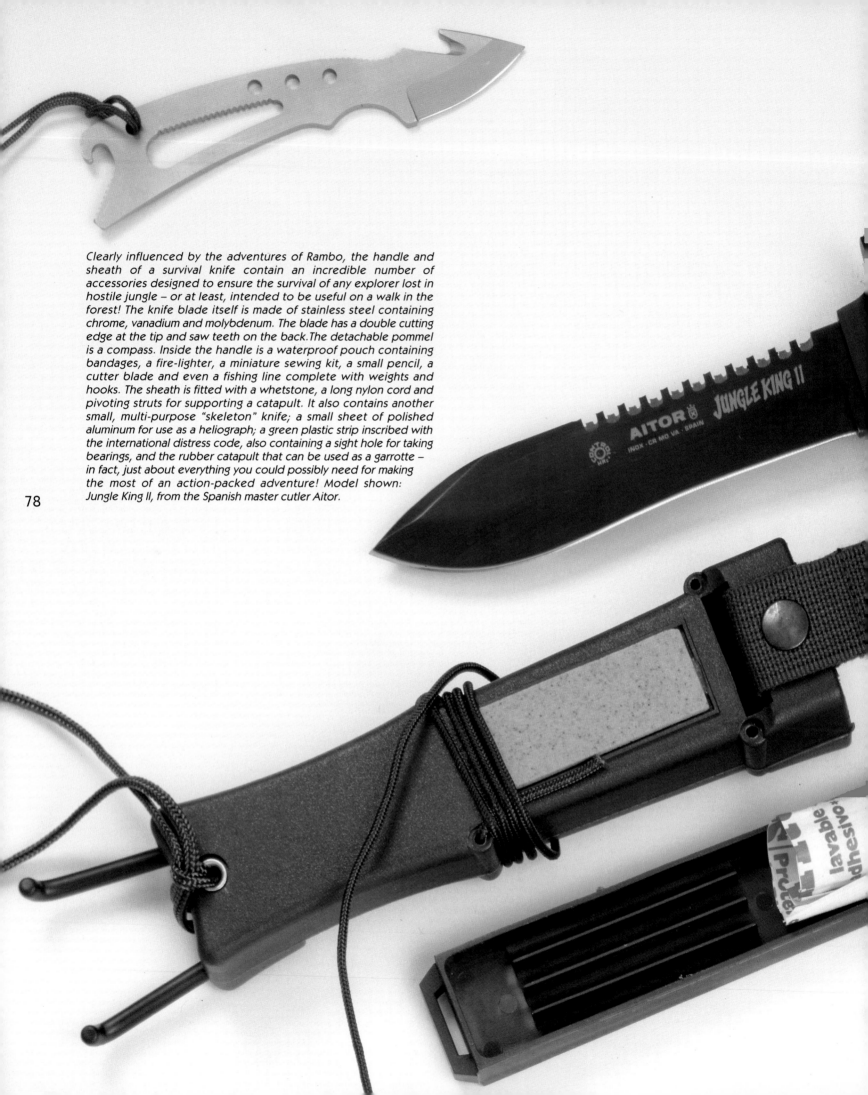

Clearly influenced by the adventures of Rambo, the handle and sheath of a survival knife contain an incredible number of accessories designed to ensure the survival of any explorer lost in hostile jungle – or at least, intended to be useful on a walk in the forest! The knife blade itself is made of stainless steel containing chrome, vanadium and molybdenum. The blade has a double cutting edge at the tip and saw teeth on the back. The detachable pommel is a compass. Inside the handle is a waterproof pouch containing bandages, a fire-lighter, a miniature sewing kit, a small pencil, a cutter blade and even a fishing line complete with weights and hooks. The sheath is fitted with a whetstone, a long nylon cord and pivoting struts for supporting a catapult. It also contains another small, multi-purpose "skeleton" knife; a small sheet of polished aluminum for use as a heliograph; a green plastic strip inscribed with the international distress code, also containing a sight hole for taking bearings, and the rubber catapult that can be used as a garrotte – in fact, just about everything you could possibly need for making the most of an action-packed adventure! Model shown: Jungle King II, from the Spanish master cutler Aitor.

78

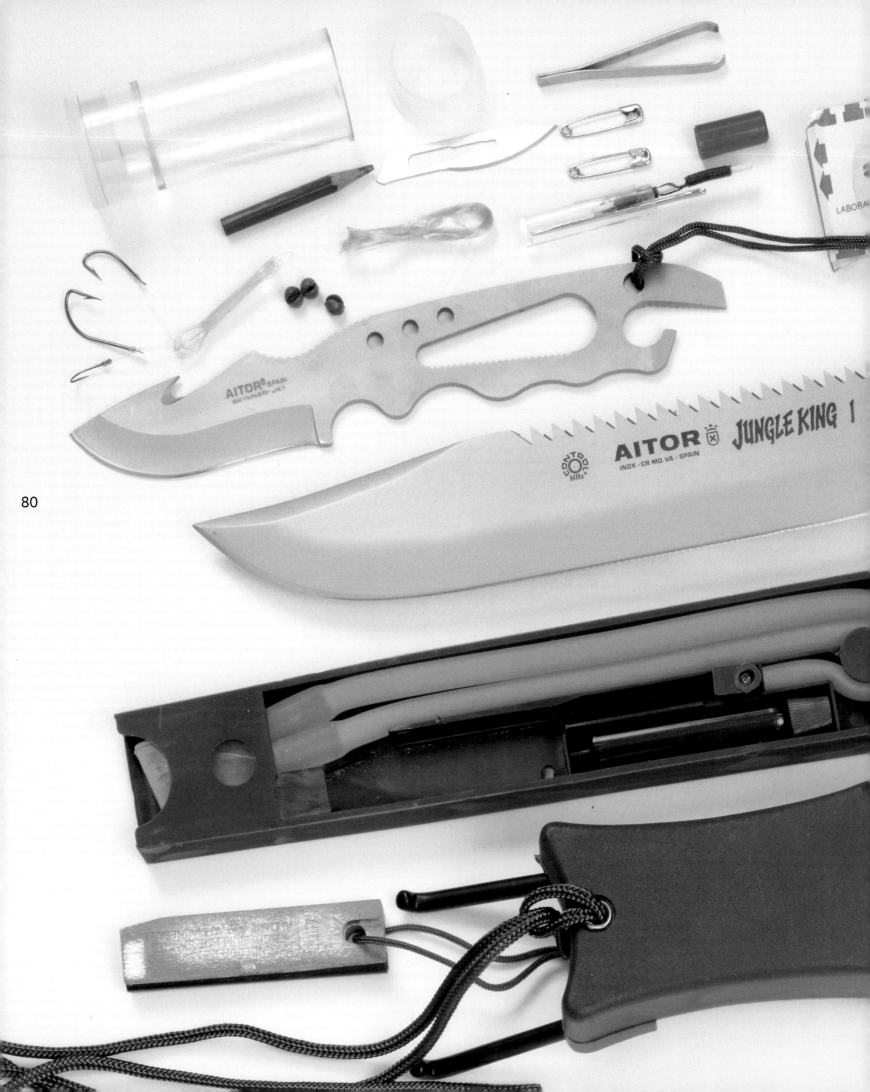

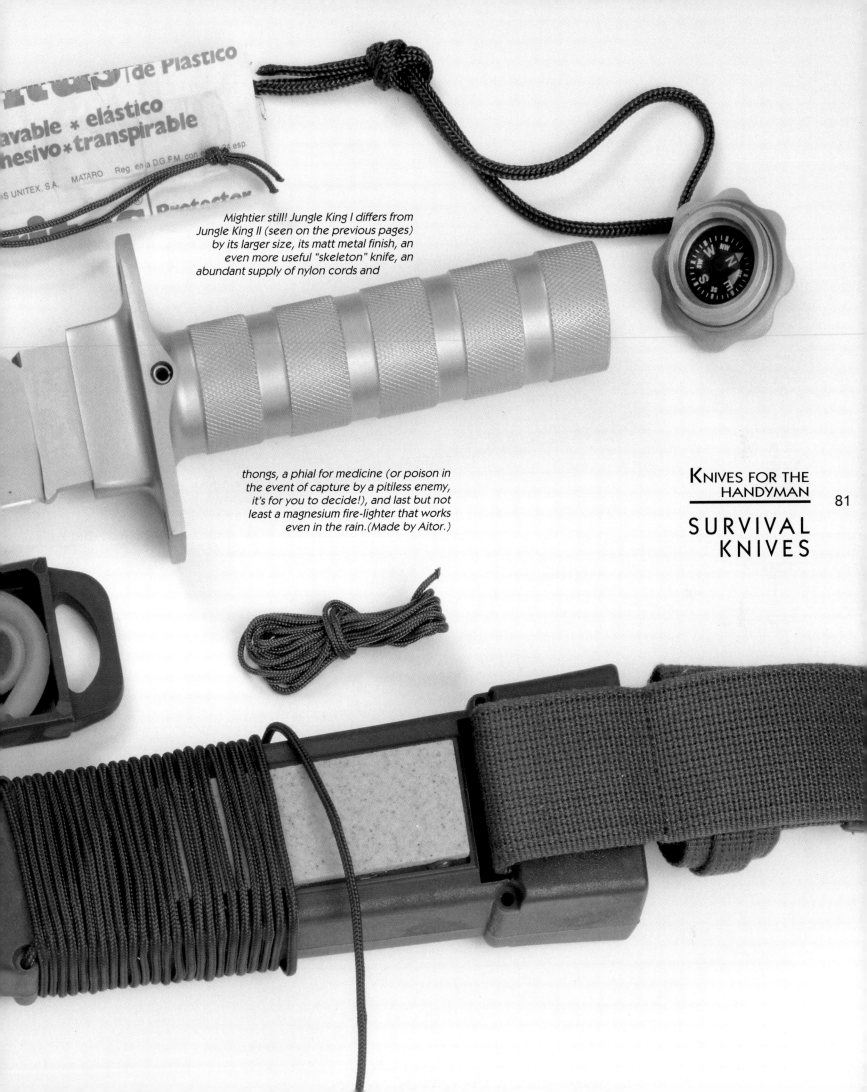

Mightier still! Jungle King I differs from Jungle King II (seen on the previous pages) by its larger size, its matt metal finish, an even more useful "skeleton" knife, an abundant supply of nylon cords and thongs, a phial for medicine (or poison in the event of capture by a pitiless enemy, it's for you to decide!), and last but not least a magnesium fire-lighter that works even in the rain. (Made by Aitor.)

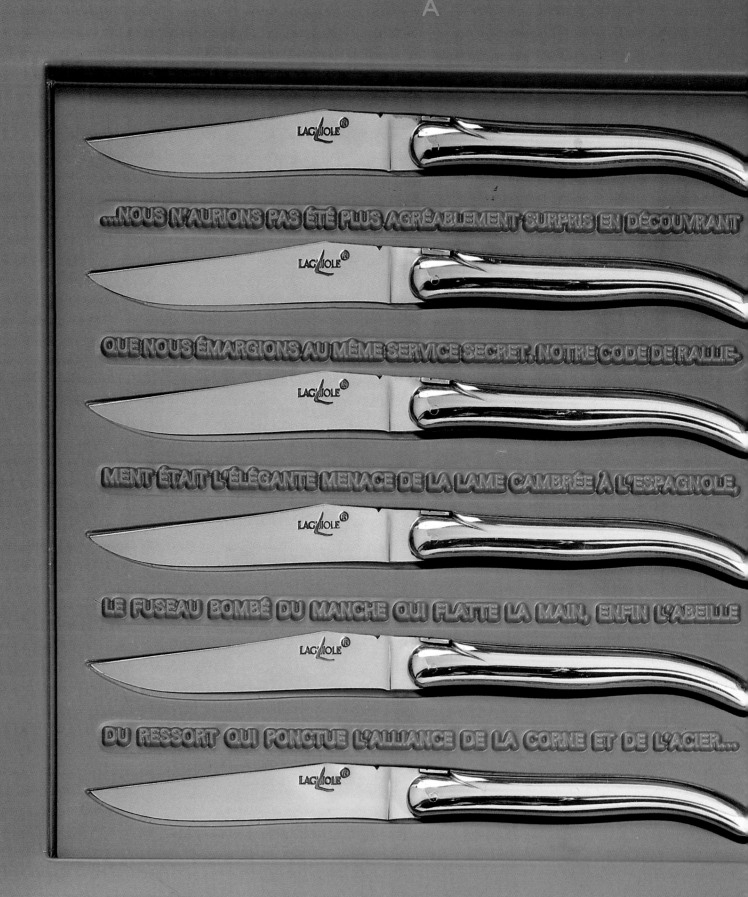

...NOUS N'AURIONS PAS ÉTÉ PLUS AGRÉABLEMENT SURPRIS EN DÉCOUVRANT

QUE NOUS ÉMARGIONS AU MÊME SERVICE SECRET. NOTRE CODE DE RALLIE-

MENT ÉTAIT L'ÉLÉGANTE MENACE DE LA LAME CAMBRÉE À L'ESPAGNOLE,

LE FUSEAU BOMBÉ DU MANCHE QUI FLATTE LA MAIN, ENFIN L'ABEILLE

DU RESSORT QUI PONCTUE L'ALLIANCE DE LA CORNE ET DE L'ACIER...

KITCHEN KNIVES

Most commonly it is in the kitchen and at the meal table that knives are used from day to day. This is all so normal and matter-of-fact that we never even give it a second thought. At the same time it shows just how inconvenient life would be without them.

Kitchen and table knives can be divided into four main categories. Take large chopping-knives first: these are used for dividing up larger items such as joints of meat, whole fish, rounds of cheese and so on. Then there are the preparing knives, such as small chopping-knives, peelers, filleting-knives and the like. There are cook's knives for cutting up various kinds of food ready for the table: bread-knives, meat-knives, fish-knives, carving-knives, etc. And fourthly we have all sorts of table knives and serving knives: steak-knives, fish-knives, fruit-knives, butter-knives, cheese-knives and the rest. Kitchen knives, because they are quite likely to be used by professionals, are above all practical, sturdy and sharp. The steel in the blade is chosen for its ability to take a keen edge with just a quick pass of the sharpening steel, and the handles are shaped to give a comfortable grip. For obvious reasons of hygiene, the knives must be easy to keep clean, and free from grooves or decorations where scraps of food could accumulate.

The table knife, on the other hand, quite naturally lends itself to the decorative arts. It is simply another item in the table setting or the domestic scene, and as such has more to do with the art of the silversmith or the goldsmith. This book therefore illustrates just a small but typical selection of traditional and contemporary styles.

83

The ErgoKnife series of so-called "sticking" knives by Pernot of Nogent (France). Stainless steel blade, plastic ergonomic handle.

84

LARGE
CHOPPING
KNIVES

Two sizes of the classic butcher's knife made by Yanip. Blades 10 inches (25 cm) stainless steel, and 13.75 inches (35 cm) indented stainless steel, respectively. Brazilian rosewood handles.

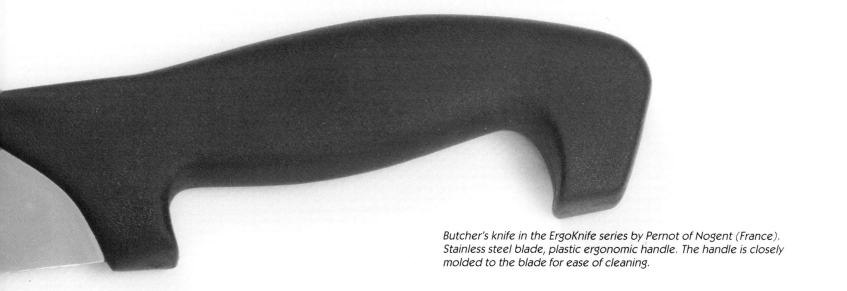

Butcher's knife in the ErgoKnife series by Pernot of Nogent (France). Stainless steel blade, plastic ergonomic handle. The handle is closely molded to the blade for ease of cleaning.

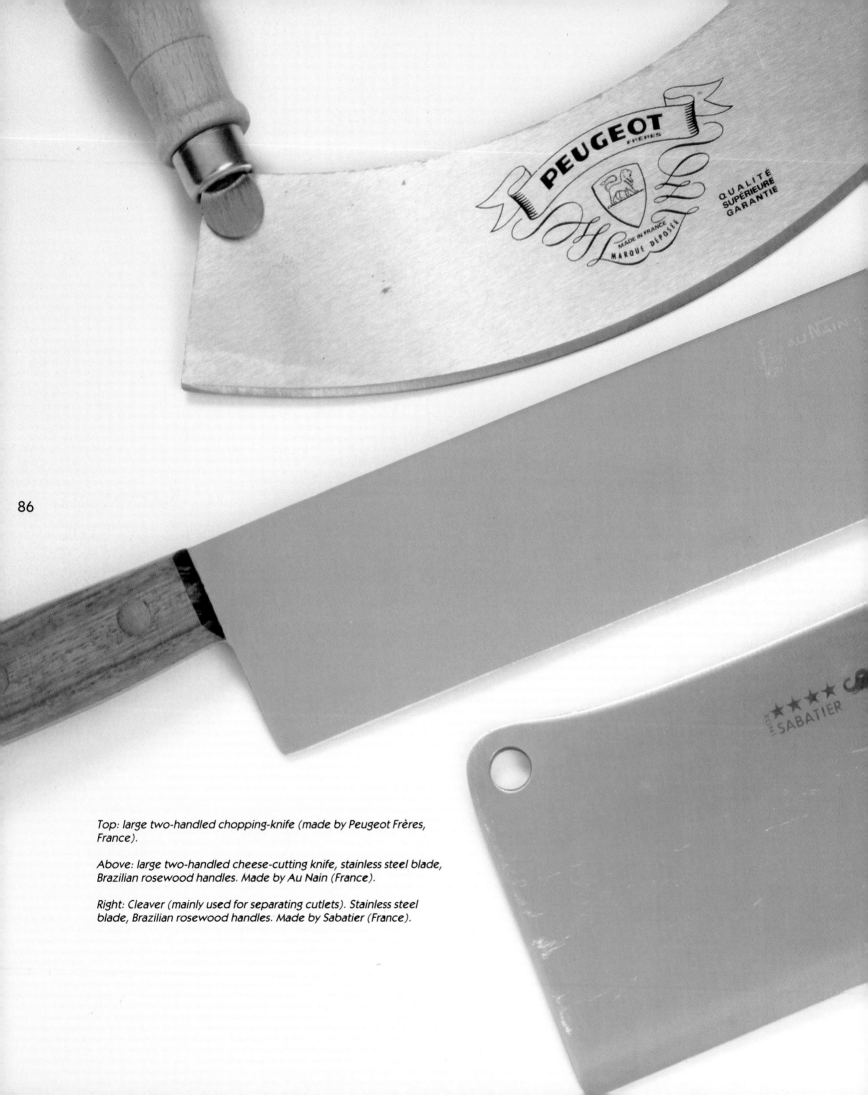

86

Top: large two-handled chopping-knife (made by Peugeot Frères, France).

Above: large two-handled cheese-cutting knife, stainless steel blade, Brazilian rosewood handles. Made by Au Nain (France).

Right: Cleaver (mainly used for separating cutlets). Stainless steel blade, Brazilian rosewood handles. Made by Sabatier (France).

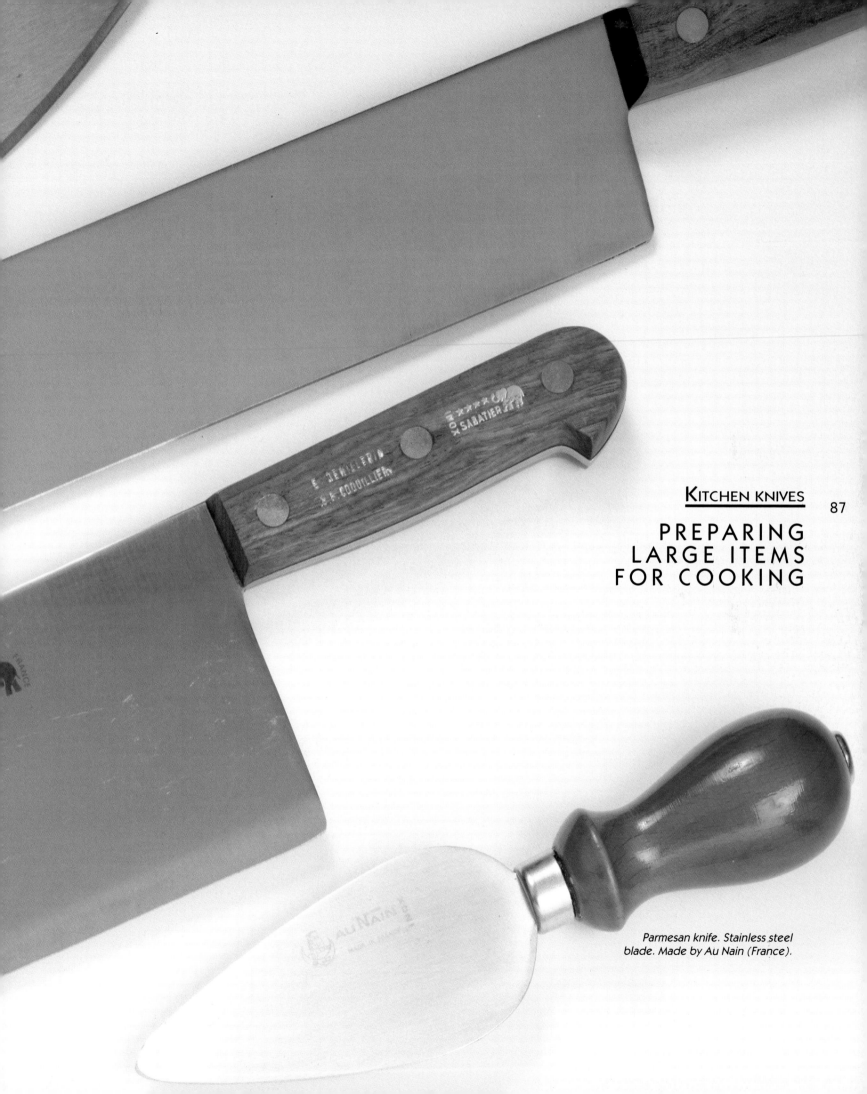

PREPARING
LARGE ITEMS
FOR COOKING

*Parmesan knife. Stainless steel
blade. Made by Au Nain (France).*

88

Right: so-called "fillet of sole" knife made of flexible stainless steel, for filleting fish.
Below: large fish-preparing knife with serrated stainless steel blade, Brazilian rosewood handle.
Made by Au Nain (France).

EHILLERIN 30
.Coquilliere

Two sizes of "chef" knives made by Yanip. Stainless steel blades.

PREPARING
COOKED
FOOD FOR
THE TABLE

Ham-boning knife with indented stainless steel blade.
Brazilian rosewood handle.

Steak knife, Brazilian rosewood handle.

A so-called "sticking" knife made by Yanip: stainless steel blade, Brazilian rosewood handle.

Bread knife made by Au Nain (France). Stainless steel blade, Brazilian rosewood handle.

PREPARING COOKED FOOD FOR THE TABLE

Tourte (pie) knife made by Deglon (France). Stainless steel blade, Brazilian rosewood handle.

Carving set. Stainless-steel bladed "Yanip" carving knife and its large, stainless steel "tuning-fork" style companion.

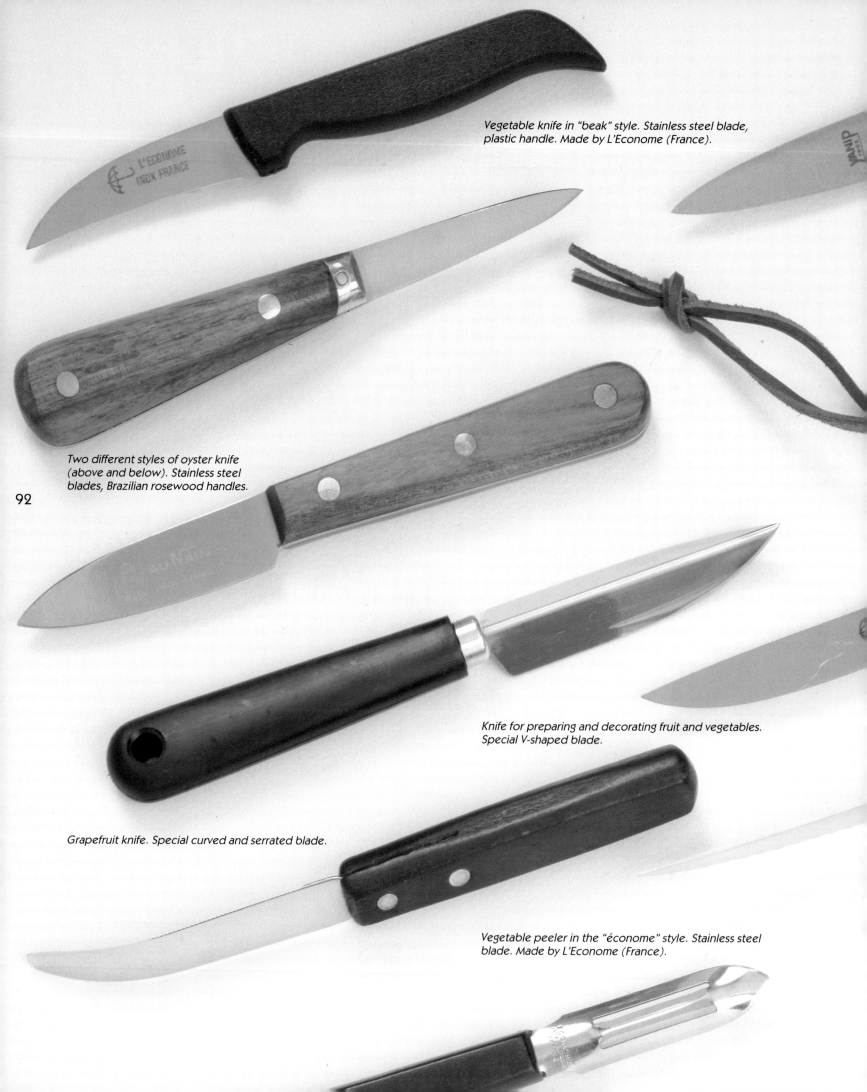

Vegetable knife in "beak" style. Stainless steel blade, plastic handle. Made by L'Econome (France).

Two different styles of oyster knife (above and below). Stainless steel blades, Brazilian rosewood handles.

92

Knife for preparing and decorating fruit and vegetables. Special V-shaped blade.

Grapefruit knife. Special curved and serrated blade.

Vegetable peeler in the "économe" style. Stainless steel blade. Made by L'Econome (France).

Pantry knife with stainless steel blade. Made by Yanip.

Small pantry knife called "chef."

Steak knife, stainless steel blade, Brazilian rosewood handle, leather thong.

FROM PANTRY TO TABLE

Steak knife, stainless steel blade, beech handle. Made by L'Econome (France).

Three steak knives with serrated stainless steel blades. Modern plastic handles (top and center) and classic wood (above). Made by Yanip.

The main difference between the "table" version of the Laguiole knife and the traditional Laguiole is its fixed blade. Because it has no pivot it can be given a 5 inch (13 cm) blade, whereas the handle is identical to the 4.7 inch (12 cm) folding knife. 440 C steel blade.

Canteen of six Laguiole table knives. Two brass bolsters, pale horn handles.

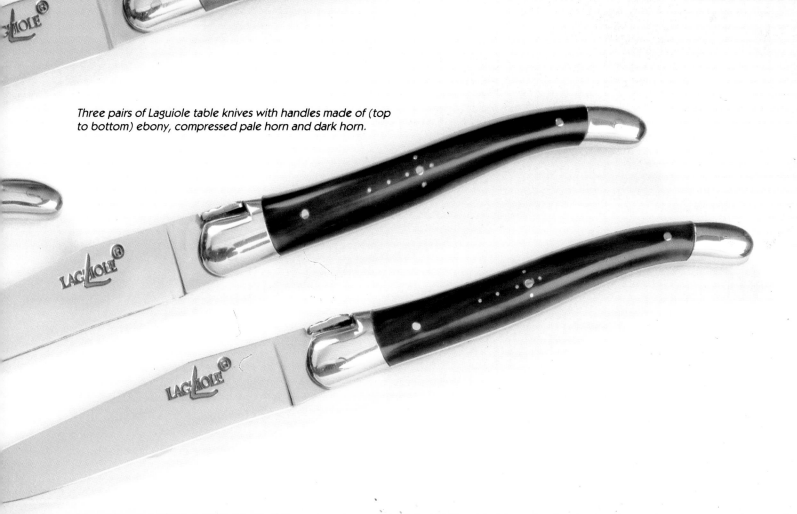

AN ALMOST RURAL SETTING

Three pairs of Laguiole table knives with handles made of (top to bottom) ebony, compressed pale horn and dark horn.

Three models in the "English" style (parallel blades with rounded ends). Stainless steel blades, special dishwasher-proof nylon handles resembling ebony, pistachio and ivory (top to bottom respectively).

96

French model inspired by the table knives of the 19th century. Stainless steel blade, horn handle and silver ferrule.

Classic French model "Vieux Paris." Solid-forged stainless steel.

Two contemporary styles in solid-forged stainless steel. Made by Henckels of Solingen (Germany).

DINNER IS SERVED M'LADY

Three original styles by Berndorf (Switzerland). Above: "Avant-garde," stainless steel blade, silver-plated handle. Below: "Windows," solid-forged stainless steel. Bottom: "Concorde," also solid-forged stainless steel.

98

Three particularly fine examples of penknife manicure sets. Stainless steel blades. Handles: tortoise-shell (top), mother-of-pearl (center) and all metal (bottom). From Nogent (France).

PENKNIVES

FLIGHTS OF AND FANCY

The penknife (or clasp knife) is by definition a small, folding pocket knife with one or more blades. Small it may be, but it can still be very handy. Some are so small they can do little more than open letters or sharpen pencils. Others may have three or even six implements: corkscrew, spike, "pen" blade (small), "pocket" blade (large), screwdriver and can/bottle-opener. Knives like these are used all the time.

There is a whole world of difference between the penknife-toolset and the mini-penknife that is more like some kind of trinket, but they all share the same high standards of styling and manufacture.

One form of specialized penknife is the manicure set. Its name suggests its main purpose. As well as a blade it always has a nail-file, and usually a pair of folding scissors.

Miniatures and other fantastical creations do not belong in the same class as their utilitarian cousins, since they are more like a collector's item or fashion accessory. Among the most intriguing flights of fancy are the Nontron miniatures, with a case made from a real walnut or hazel-nut shell containing up to twelve genuine folding knives! First dreamed up in 1849 as masterpieces for craftsmen to prove their skills, these knives became so popular that they are still produced in large numbers. On the other hand, another piece from the master cutlers of Nontron has remained unique: a set of ten minute knives inside a cherry stone!

These knives are shown larger than actual size.

Four traditionally styled penknives. From the top down: stainless steel manicure set; stainless steel penknife; horn-handled three-piece penknife; ivory-handled two-piece penknife (made in France).

German penknife manicure set made in Solingen. Arginox handle, stainless steel blade.

Multi-purpose penknife with stainless steel blade.

Swedish three-piece penknife made by Eka.

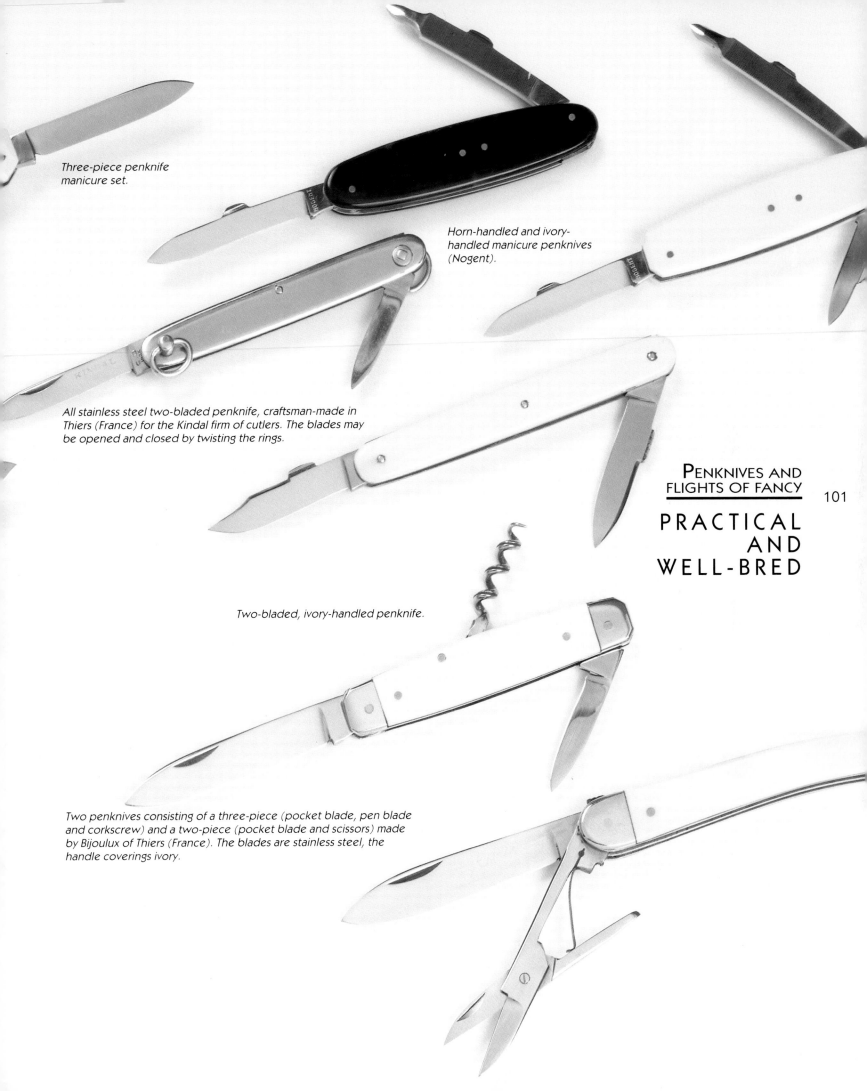

Three-piece penknife
manicure set.

Horn-handled and ivory-
handled manicure penknives
(Nogent).

All stainless steel two-bladed penknife, craftsman-made in
Thiers (France) for the Kindal firm of cutlers. The blades may
be opened and closed by twisting the rings.

PRACTICAL
AND
WELL-BRED

Two-bladed, ivory-handled penknife.

Two penknives consisting of a three-piece (pocket blade, pen blade
and corkscrew) and a two-piece (pocket blade and scissors) made
by Bijoulux of Thiers (France). The blades are stainless steel, the
handle coverings ivory.

All stainless steel manicure penknife.

102

Circular key-ring manicure set made by Éloi (France), housed in an authentic silver Five-Franc piece.

Two key-ring manicure sets by E. Drouhin of Nogent (France). The handle coverings are (upper) briar root and (lower) deer horn.

Two very fine circular manicure sets, also from E. Drouhin. The coverings are horn on the left, tortoise-shell on the right.

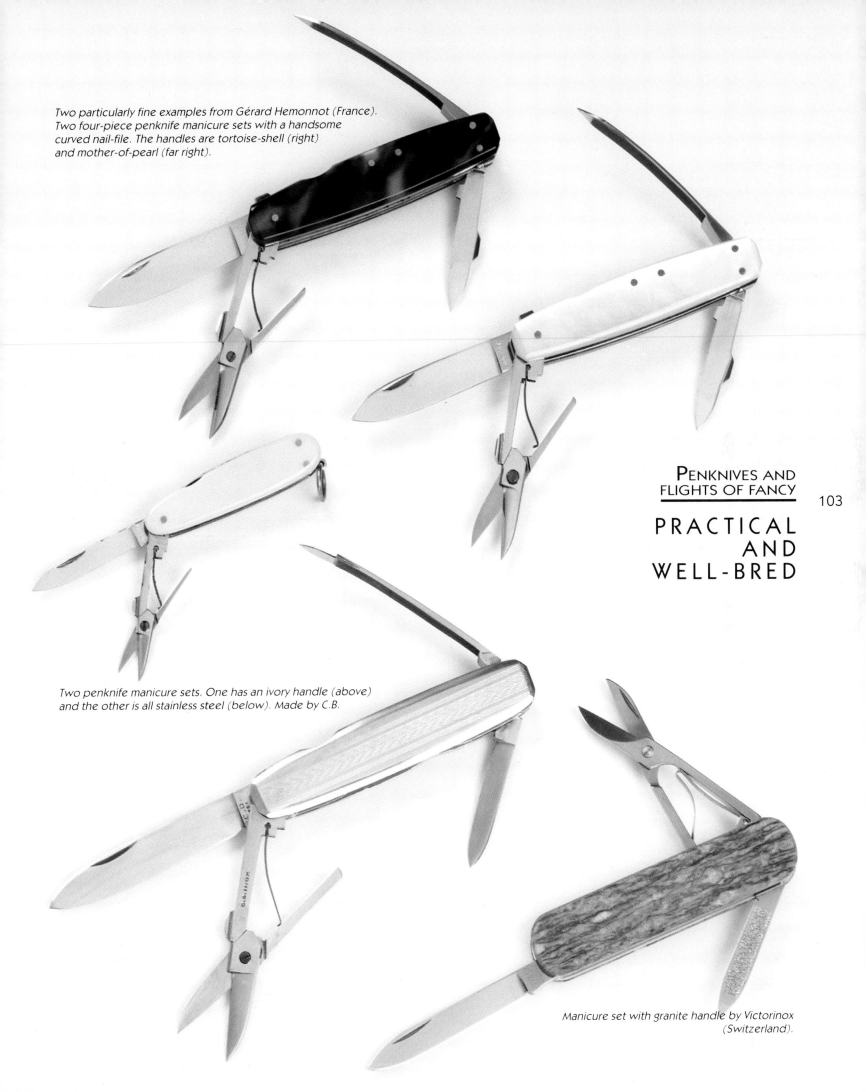

Two particularly fine examples from Gérard Hemonnot (France).
Two four-piece penknife manicure sets with a handsome
curved nail-file. The handles are tortoise-shell (right)
and mother-of-pearl (far right).

PENKNIVES AND
FLIGHTS OF FANCY

103

PRACTICAL
AND
WELL-BRED

Two penknife manicure sets. One has an ivory handle (above)
and the other is all stainless steel (below). Made by C.B.

Manicure set with granite handle by Victorinox
(Switzerland).

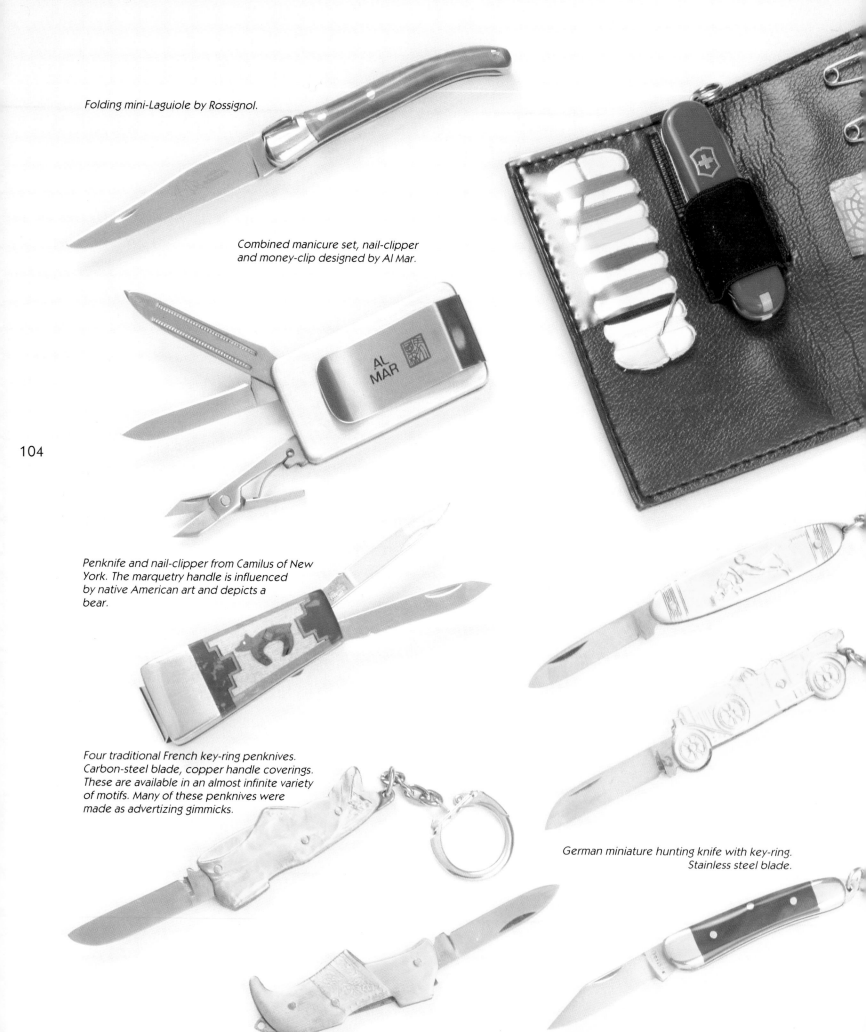

Folding mini-Laguiole by Rossignol.

Combined manicure set, nail-clipper and money-clip designed by Al Mar.

AL MAR

104

Penknife and nail-clipper from Camilus of New York. The marquetry handle is influenced by native American art and depicts a bear.

Four traditional French key-ring penknives. Carbon-steel blade, copper handle coverings. These are available in an almost infinite variety of motifs. Many of these penknives were made as advertizing gimmicks.

German miniature hunting knife with key-ring. Stainless steel blade.

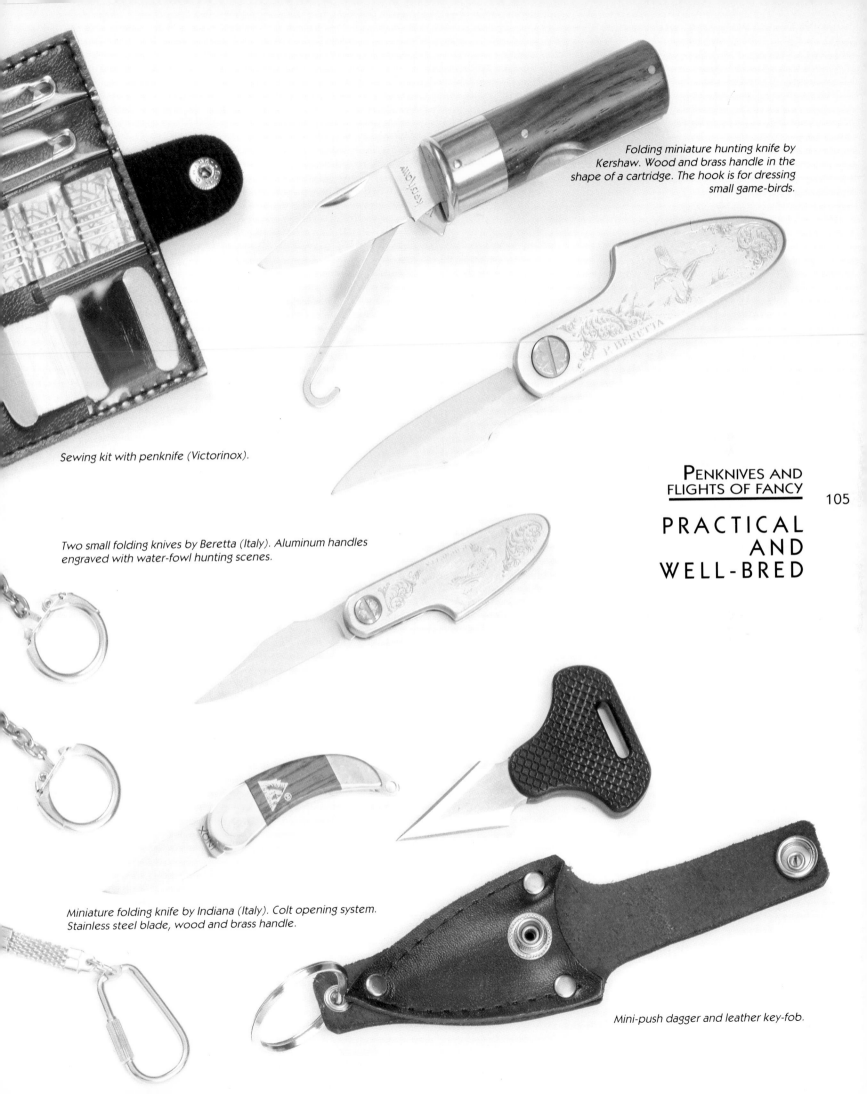

Folding miniature hunting knife by Kershaw. Wood and brass handle in the shape of a cartridge. The hook is for dressing small game-birds.

Sewing kit with penknife (Victorinox).

PENKNIVES AND
FLIGHTS OF FANCY

105

PRACTICAL
AND
WELL-BRED

Two small folding knives by Beretta (Italy). Aluminum handles engraved with water-fowl hunting scenes.

Miniature folding knife by Indiana (Italy). Colt opening system. Stainless steel blade, wood and brass handle.

Mini-push dagger and leather key-fob.

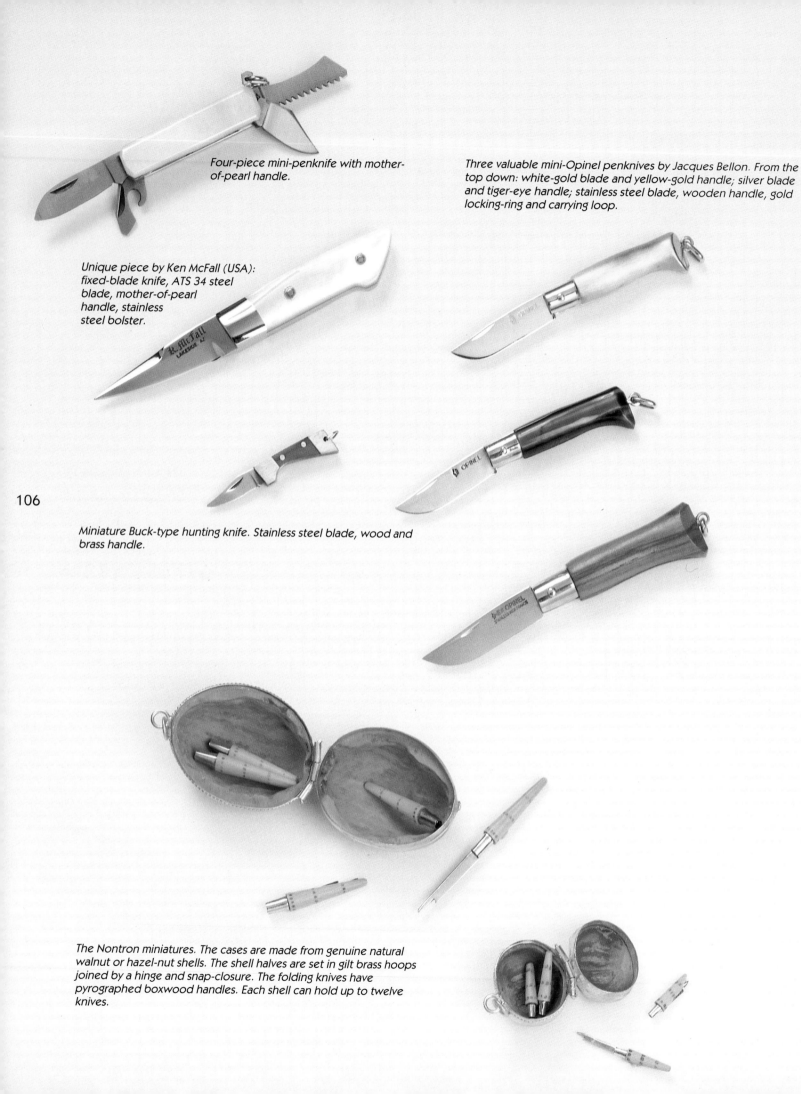

Four-piece mini-penknife with mother-of-pearl handle.

Three valuable mini-Opinel penknives by Jacques Bellon. From the top down: white-gold blade and yellow-gold handle; silver blade and tiger-eye handle; stainless steel blade, wooden handle, gold locking-ring and carrying loop.

Unique piece by Ken McFall (USA): fixed-blade knife, ATS 34 steel blade, mother-of-pearl handle, stainless steel bolster.

Miniature Buck-type hunting knife. Stainless steel blade, wood and brass handle.

The Nontron miniatures. The cases are made from genuine natural walnut or hazel-nut shells. The shell halves are set in gilt brass hoops joined by a hinge and snap-closure. The folding knives have pyrographed boxwood handles. Each shell can hold up to twelve knives.

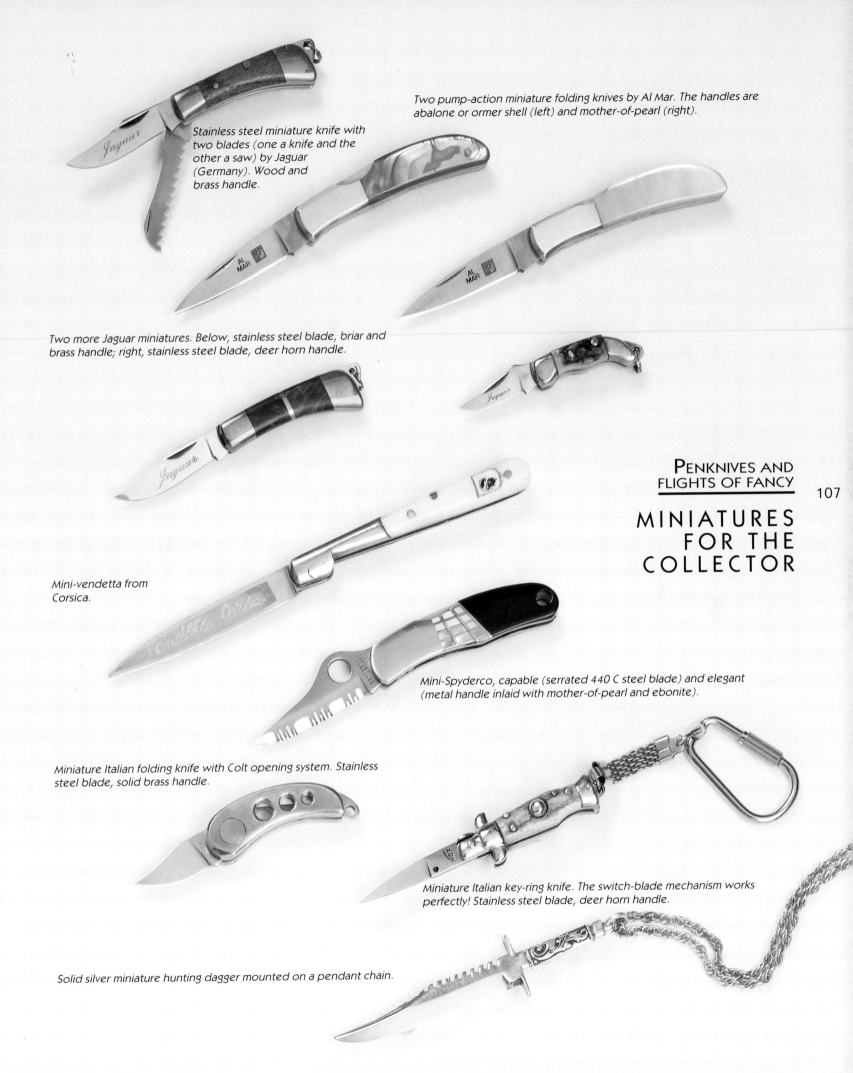

Stainless steel miniature knife with two blades (one a knife and the other a saw) by Jaguar (Germany). Wood and brass handle.

Two pump-action miniature folding knives by Al Mar. The handles are abalone or ormer shell (left) and mother-of-pearl (right).

Two more Jaguar miniatures. Below, stainless steel blade, briar and brass handle; right, stainless steel blade, deer horn handle.

Mini-vendetta from Corsica.

Mini-Spyderco, capable (serrated 440 C steel blade) and elegant (metal handle inlaid with mother-of-pearl and ebonite).

Miniature Italian folding knife with Colt opening system. Stainless steel blade, solid brass handle.

Miniature Italian key-ring knife. The switch-blade mechanism works perfectly! Stainless steel blade, deer horn handle.

Solid silver miniature hunting dagger mounted on a pendant chain.

Created exclusively for Kindal, this knife is influenced by the traditional "skinner", with 576-layer Damascus blade, nickel silver guard. The solid rosewood handle provides an excellent grip.

108

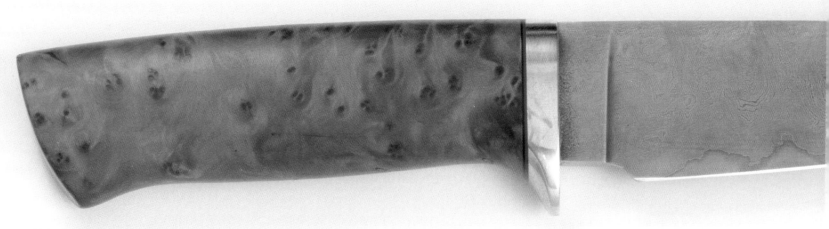

Knife in hunting style by Henry Viallon (France). Damascus blade, nickel silver mini-guard, bur elm handle.

UNUSUAL KNIVES

As with quantity production, so the tradition of the entirely hand-made knife has been steadily regaining in strength since the early twentieth century.

This movement was started by the American William Scagell (1872-1963), who first set up as a craftsman in 1910. At that time Scagell was known to just a few hunters and trappers in his locality. They valued the strength of his hand-forged blades, and the handles made of banded leather and deer horn. Now, collectors will pay high prices for them. A Scagell knife that would have cost some $20 around 1960 would today fetch over $6,000.

109

The movement spread outward from the USA to the entire world. Many a blacksmith has rediscovered the secret of making Damascus steel. The technique consists of melting and fusing iron and steel bars, then hammering the resulting block, folding it back on itself and forming alternating layers of the different metals. The Damascus bar is then polished and dipped in acid, revealing a pattern that is never the same twice.

Although most craftsmen still work with traditional materials (steel, wood, ivory, leather, and the like), some are turning toward avant-garde materials such as titanium and fine ceramics. Fine ceramics are quite revolutionary, and such knives, even those made in quantity, are still in a special class of their own.

These knives are shown larger than actual size.

Knife by Pierre Reverdy (France) with a triple-twist, 1024-layer Damascus blade. Bronze guard. Handle made of Arizona ironwood and green-dyed deer horn, nickel silver pommel, sharkskin-clad limewood stock.

Knife by Embratsen (Sweden). L6 carbon-nickel steel blade forged as two 160-layer blocks. Deer horn blade.

110

Combat knife by Jim Ence (USA). Damascus steel blade, deer horn handle, bolster of 1500-layer Damascus steel inlaid with gilt leaves.

Full Damascus folding knife by Khalsa (USA). Carbon-steel blade, carbon-nickel handle.

"Passion" knife by Pierre Reverdy (France). Damascus blade with 56-layer nickel steel outside and K 720 steel core. Bronze guard, deer horn handle. Hand-sewn Madras goatskin sheath (not shown).

THE SPLENDOR OF DAMASCUS STEEL

Folder hunting knife by Tommy Lee (USA). The blade and spring are Damascus steel. Titanium linings engraved by Mel Wood. Ivory handle.

Knife by Michel Blum (France). Forged Damascus steel blade by Rados (USA). Engraved silver bolster and pommel. The handle is made of oosik (fossilized walrus penis). The scabbard (not illustrated) is made of sharkskin.

"Pebble" knife by Daniel Tardy (France). Reindeer antler handle with scrimshaw engraving.

The word "scrimshaw" does not refer to a type of knife, but to the technique of engraving on bone or ivory (nowadays also on high-quality synthetic materials such as micarta).

This art form originated among the Eskimos. American seafarers first discovered it on whaling expeditions in the early 19th century and took it up as a way of passing the time.

The tradition long remained local to the northeastern seaboard of the USA, in particular New England, and the designs had mainly a nautical theme.

Decorated knife handles were just a fraction of the total scrimshaw output, the rest being devoted to ornamental objects or the butt-plates of firearms. Due to present restrictions on the trade in ivory, scrimshanders are increasingly using fossil ivory (especially mammoth tusk), buffalo horn or synthetic materials, and the results are often quite remarkable.

Since each engraving is carried out by hand, it goes without saying that every knife decorated with scrimshaw is unique.

Hunting knife made by Puma (Germany). Series commemorating the five-hundredth anniversary of the discovery of America by Christopher Columbus, part of a limited edition of fifty only (the knife shown here is number 2). Scrimshaw by Arno Hopp on ivory-style micarta. The other side of the handle is a scrimshaw depiction of the course Columbus followed across the Atlantic.

Another example of Arno Hopp's scrimshaw technique on ivory-style micarta, also for a hunting knife by Puma.

Hunting knife made by Boker (Germany). The handle decoration is a bas-relief engraving (not scrimshaw) on ivory-style micarta. The other side depicts a bison.

Close combat knife by Tommy Lee (USA): 440 C steel blade. Handle decorated with a scrimshaw by Bob Burdette entitled "Eagle."

THE ART OF SCRIMSHAW

Small hunting knife by R.B. Johnson (USA): 440 C steel blade. Handle decorated with a scrimshaw by Denise Kondula on mammoth ivory.

"Drop point" knife by Reddiex. ATS 34 steel blade, 416 S stainless steel bolster. Scrimshaw by S. Holland on ivory-style micarta.

A superb knife by Larry Fuegen (USA) with a Damascus steel blade and burnished steel guard. The sheath is tooled lizard skin.

114

The blade and handle are forged from a single piece of steel on this knife from Charles M. Roulin (Switzerland). The mammoth is sculpted in the solid metal. The handle coverings are ebony with micarta linings and three floral rivets.

Knife in the "tanto" style by Jacques Jobin (Canada). The Damascus steel blade was forged by Darryl Meier, the handle and sheath were sculpted in amourette wood by José di Bregno. Conventionally assembled with solid silver fittings.

Close combat knife from D. Beaver (USA): 440 C steel blade. Tiger coral handle, titanium bolsters, engravings by Judy Beaver.

THE ART OF THE MASTER CRAFTSMAN

Dagger by Friedly (USA). ATS 34 steel blade. Handle and sheath of fossilized walrus ivory. The handle is inlaid with a solid silver spiral.

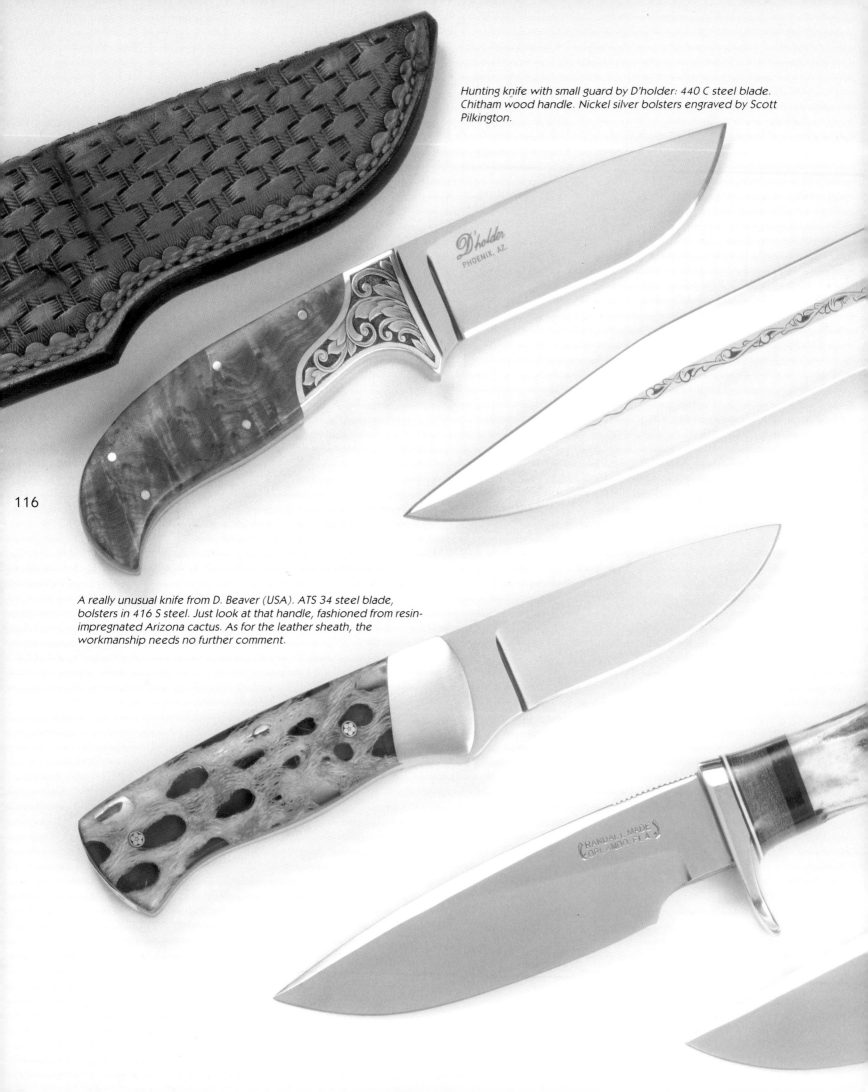

Hunting knife with small guard by D'holder: 440 C steel blade. Chitham wood handle. Nickel silver bolsters engraved by Scott Pilkington.

116

A really unusual knife from D. Beaver (USA). ATS 34 steel blade, bolsters in 416 S steel. Just look at that handle, fashioned from resin-impregnated Arizona cactus. As for the leather sheath, the workmanship needs no further comment.

Dagger by Tommy Lee (USA): 440 C steel blade and deer horn handle. Superbly engraved blade and bolster.

THE ART OF THE MASTER CRAFTSMAN

Two sizes of "trapper" knife (5-inch and 6-inch) from Randall. Swedish carbon-steel blades, nickel silver guards. Deer horn and banded leather handles, duralumin pommel.

"Gentleman's side lock folder" from D. Beaver (USA). Damascus steel blade by Fain Edwards. Nickel fixings. Nickel handle with silver coverings engraved by Judy Beaver.

"Liner lock" folding knife by Wolf Borger (Germany). CPMT 440 V special steel blade. Anodized titanium bolsters. The handle linings are also made of titanium, with micarta coverings. The knife can be fully dismantled.

118

"Liner lock" folding knife by D. Beaver (USA): ATS 34 steel blade. Anodized titanium handle engraved by Judy Beaver.

Two "pebble" knives by Daniel Tardy (France) made of solid Brazilian rosewood (above) and bird's-eye maple (right).

Another fine example of a knife on an animal theme from Pascal Barbet (France). This is called "The Swallow." 440 C steel blade, ebony and elephant ivory handle. Notice how beautifully the sheath has been cut away to match the swallow's outline.

"Baby tanto" by Ray Bears (USA): 440 C steel blade. Lace wood handle and sheath. Nickel and silver bolster hoop.

"Serpent" knife by Pascal Barbet (France): 440 C steel blade. The ebony handle is inlaid with ivory, the gilt snake's head has a coral tongue, ivory fangs and jade eyes.

THE ART OF THE MASTER CRAFTSMAN

"Drop point" knife by Cheatham (USA). The blade has been treated to resemble flint. Nickel silver guard, cocuswood handle.

"Peanut" knife by D'holder (USA), with 440 C steel blade, titanium handle coverings with an ornamental layer of wild sheep horn.

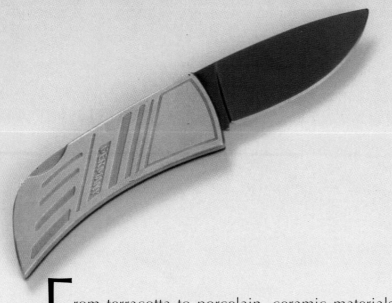

From terracotta to porcelain, ceramic materials have been familiar to us for thousands of years. Now, as a spin-off from space research, modern high technology has been reappraising these materials, and they are proving to have qualities of hardness, sharpness and durability that greatly surpass even those of steel. They are used in a wide variety of applications, including the automotive and aerospace industries, surgical prosthetics, office automation and, naturally, cutlery.

Fine ceramics are ultra-fine powders with a particle size of less than a micron (under one thousandth of a millimetre, or less than four one-hundred thousandths of an inch). To produce knife blades, these micro-crystals of metallic oxides are compressed, sintered (vitrified) at high temperature and then machined on a diamond wheel.

Such blades have a hardness index of 7 to 9, making them almost as hard as diamond (hardness index 10), and four to five times harder than the finest steel.

At the present time two techniques exist side by side. The all-ceramic blades are made of zircon (zirconium oxide). These are white or black and the cutting edge is almost impossible to dull. Then there are steel blades coated with a thin layer of titanium nitride (golden in color) or titanium carbonitride (black).

Top: small German folding knife with zircon blade. Above right: zircon-bladed chopping knife; black, dishwasher-safe, special ABS plastic handle.
Right: folding knife, black zircon blade, solid aluminum handle. The blade is released by pressing the button on the pivot-joint.

120

Left: chopping-knife with a steel blade coated with titanium nitride.
Compressed wood handle. Below: the same knife with a multi-layer
coating of titanium nitride and titanium carbonitride.

FINE CERAMICS IN THE NEW STONE AGE

Chef's knife: steel blade coated with titanium nitride and titanium
carbonitride, compressed wood handle.

122

Two contemporary interpretations of the famous Scandinavian knife, signed by J. Henriksen. This Danish craftsman is also an engineer specializing in fine ceramics. The overall effect superbly combines the traditional and the modern. The blades are solid zircon and the handles make use of traditional materials. The upper example has a buffalo horn and walrus bone handle. The handle on the lower one is made of fossilized bog oak with banded leather decorations.

Tradition meets high technology. Three styles from Éloi and two from Laguiole, made by Brossard; all blades coated with titanium carbonitride (courtesy GTI).
A supreme touch of refinement: the circle set into the middle of the Éloi handle (right) will take a precious or semi-precious stone of the owner's choosing.

FINE
CERAMICS
IN THE NEW
STONE AGE

COLLECTING KNIVES

Knife collectors are rather scarce in Europe, unlike North America, and in particular the United States. It was a long-established tradition in rural areas of Europe that you only had one knife, and you only bought a new one when your old one was definitely worn out or lost. Four knives in an entire lifetime was a lot!

Yet knives are among the most attractive and varied objects you could imagine, especially now that the craftsman movement has become firmly established. Imports of foreign-manufactured knives are on the increase, and the traditional patterns are arousing a great deal of interest.

So the only question is: which knives to collect? As with any kind of collection, rule number one is to do what you enjoy. Some collect only combat knives, others stay with the pocket knife (of which there must be tens of thousands of different kinds), while still others specialize in the work of one or more master craftsmen. Or you might prefer to collect penknives, gadget-knives, knives with scrimshaw on them, or perhaps those with the most unusual opening and locking systems. Earlier

A unique and most unusual piece: "The Howler," one of the masterpieces in the monster range by Larry Fuegen. "The Howler" symbolizes the god of hurricanes. Here it is shown in side view (facing page) and end-on to the sculpted pommel (above).

This knife is shown larger than actual size.

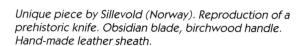

Unique piece by Sillevold (Norway). Reproduction of a prehistoric knife. Obsidian blade, birchwood handle. Hand-made leather sheath.

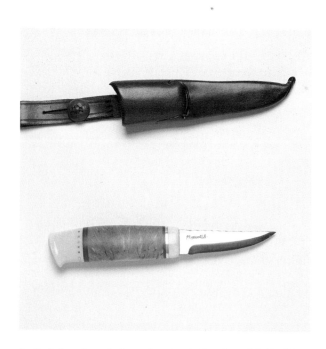

Entirely hand-made Scandinavian knife, signed E. Havlid, with sheath.

chapters will have given you food for thought about the kind of collection you might like to build. Even so, it is only an overview of what is happening on the contemporary scene, and there are plenty of other patterns, brand-names and craftsmen in the market-place. A visit to a cutlery store or gunsmith's will give you a fuller picture.

The list of possible themes is almost endless, and you do not need a fortune to start collecting. For a few dollars you can easily get a shepherd's knife or penknife of unusual design, and out-of-town market stalls are a rich source for anyone with an eagle eye.

Having said that, fine knives are expensive, some even very expensive. Larry Fuegen's "The Howler," for instance, costs close on $7,000. Since it takes a master craftsman the better part of three months full time work to produce such a piece, that is not at all unreasonable – even though it may be out of most people's reach.

Staying for a moment with the financial aspect of knife collecting, craftsman-made pieces can be an attractive investment. For one thing, even with knives produced in limited quantities (a few hundred at most) the fact that they are put together by hand means that each knife is subtly different from all the others. Then again, the quoted prices for the output of a particular artist are likely to rise after that person's death. In the case of a knife by the late Bill Scagell (died 1963) worth around $20 in the 1960s, the price today is closer to $6,000.

Matching pairs of knives also represent good value. They are two knives of different types, but produced by the same cutler in the same materials and style. Matching pairs are relatively scarce, and a "must" for any collection.

No matter what area you decide to specialize in, you can always choose to buy on impulse when you see something you like, or to collect thematically on a systematic, fully-documented basis. What you decide does not matter, so long as you are pleased with the result.

So it is up to you to build your personal collection of knives that really please you. In the words of Siméon Busquère, a famous French collector: "A knife is a mirror of the heart. You can discover intelligence and goodness, or stupidity and even malice, in a knife."

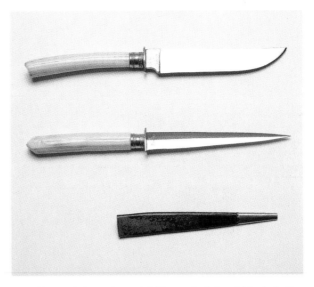

Matching pair from Antonini (France). A fixed-blade knife with a stiletto and sheath.

Knife with Damascus steel blade by Hank Knickmeyer (USA). Hippopotamus tusk handle.

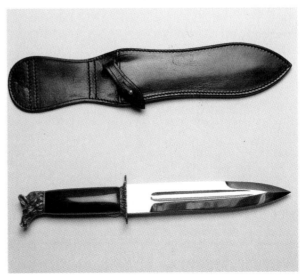

Hunting dagger by Lefaucheux. Blade by Mongin (La Maison des Couteliers), bronze guard and pommel, buffalo horn haft.

128

Pair of monsters by Larry Fuegen (USA). A sea monster, "Sea No Evil," right, and "The Howler," depicting a hurricane, facing page. Folding knives without locking-notch, 360-layer Damascus steel blades, fully sculpted stag-antler handles.

The handle of "The Howler" is albino deer horn. The monsters' eyes are semi-precious stones. Their tongues are free to move. Twisted ivory decorates the inside of the blade housings. The bases are clumps of mineral on rare wood plinths. Each bears a plate engraved with the name of the knife. Quite clearly unique!

129

KEEPING KNIVES IN GOOD CONDITION

Strangely, the less a knife is used the more it deteriorates. It will tarnish, jam in various ways, the wood will dry out, and so on. But a knife used regularly also needs regular attention. Here are the essentials of what to do in order to keep a knife in perfect condition for a very long time.

MAINTAINING THE BLADE

The most basic piece of maintenance is of course sharpening. This needs to be done with a steady hand, or your knife may cut less well than before.

Sharpening with the steel: this is a very fast way. It is what a butcher does before cutting a steak. This is practical and effective for kitchen and table knives, but is definitely not for hunting or combat knives, whether the steel is the traditional or diamond kind.

With its scored, pitted blade and dull, lifeless handle, this neglected knife could use an overhaul! (private collection) (above). Two water-lubricated whetstones in carrying-cases (below).

Sharpening with the whetstone: this is the oldest way, but also requires the most skill. The angle at which the cutting edge is sharpened must be uniform and symmetrical along the whole blade, which is easier said than done.

The whetstone must be lubricated with water or cutting oil, depending on type. The ideal situation is to have three stones, one medium and one coarse for blade overhauls, and one fine for day-to-day upkeep. If you are not a virtuoso of the whetstone, the "Lansky Sharpener" is the safest way. This is a simple whetstone guidance system and gives you the correct sharpening angle first time, every time.

Oil whetstones (boxed Gatco stone and a Japanese stone). Puma cutting oil.

Shown larger than actual size.

Diamond sharpeners, including a pocket version with double folding handle like a butterfly knife.

Large, oval, professional-quality steel for sharpening chefs' and butchers' knives.

Three small steels for home use, including a special mini-steel for penknives.

Ceramic sharpeners: hold the sharpener by the handle and move the knife blade smoothly forward and back along the ceramic rods. This is a gentle and not particularly difficult method.

Diamond sharpeners: these are highly portable and easy to use in the open air. They are impregnated with diamond dust and need to be lubricated with water. The fine grades will give razor sharpness.

Tarnish removal: even with stainless steel a blade always loses its brightness in the end. Never clean it with a pot-scourer, as the polished finish will be ruined. The best method is to use steel wool impregnated with gun oil and stroke gently in the direction of polish. This method also works for bronzed blades.

If the blade is pitted with rust, the only answer is to use a piece of cotton impregnated with Puma polishing paste.

MAINTAINING THE HANDLE

The metal parts: clean these using the same methods and materials as blades. Brass bolsters can be brightened up again by rubbing them over with a soft cloth moistened in wine vinegar. Aluminum bolsters should be gently repolished with dry steel wool.

Handle coverings: metal handles should be maintained in the same way as blades and bolsters. Unvarnished wooden handles will look better for linseed oil or beeswax applied with a woollen cloth. The boxwood handles of Nontron knives just soak up foie gras grease! Horn handles need no maintenance, but do remember that horn must never be immersed in water, especially hot water, which will distort it beyond repair.

Maintenance of any kind on coverings of stone, ivory, tortoise-shell or bone should be done only by a professional.

HANDY TIPS

• Never store a knife in a leather sheath. The tanning chemicals are acidic and would soon tarnish it badly.

• If a knife is used only rarely, coat it in gun oil or wipe it with a rust-inhibiting cloth, or coat it with a film of water-repellent gel (silicon type), and wrap it in a plastic bag (a freezer bag is ideal).

• A drop of mineral oil on the pivot joint of a folding or multi-purpose knife is always useful.

• Never rub a blade with emery cloth or glass-paper, and never attempt to sharpen it yourself with a grindstone.

• When lubricating a whetstone (with oil or water), do not flood it. A few drops are enough!

• Before buying any kind of sharpener, get advice from the retailer and ask for a demonstration.

• If you have the slightest doubt about your ability to sharpen or maintain a knife correctly, give the job to a professional rather than risk ruining it for all time.

Sharpener made of ceramic rods in a wooden base.

"Lansky Sharpener" kit with its three oilstones on plastic stands, stone-guiding rods and blade-grip marked with sharpening angles.

COLLECTORS' KNIVES – AT ANY PRICE?

Collectors' knives are not the subject of feverish market speculation. Prices stay within reasonable bounds and climb slowly but surely in relation to the age, condition and rarity of the piece. Prices for different examples of the same type of knife still being manufactured relate to the production variants that specialists spend their time noticing and documenting. This means that when you are buying a pre-owned knife you need to have a sound knowledge of the subject, particularly if a substantial sum of money is involved – unless you hear that small inner voice that dealers know so well, insistently telling you here is a bargain not to be missed!

Below, for guidance, are the main market prices reached in the United States for the Buck 110 hunting knife folder that has been in production since 1963:

Version 1: type 1, 1963: $600. Type 2, 1964: $500. Type 3, 1964/65: $400. Type 4, 1964/65: $500.

Version 2: type 1, 1965/66: $250. Type 2, 1966/68: $175. Type 3, 1968/70: $150. Type 4, 1970: $150.

Version 3: type 1, 1970: $200. Type 2, 1971: $150. Type 3, 1971/73: $125.

Version 4: type 1, 1973/78: $100. Type 2, 1978/80: $75. Type 3a, 1980/82: $60. Type 3b, 1982/83: $60. Type 3c, 1983/86: $55.

Conclusion: you may not make your fortune collecting knives, but at least you are sure not just to hold your capital value, but actually to see regular capital growth. Not all collectors can say the same!

Some examples of collectable present-day knives. From left to right, Victorinox Swiss Army knife, Lee close combat knife (USA), Scandinavian knife (signed J.G.), knife with Damascus steel blade by Herbertz (Germany), reproduction prehistoric knife by Ginelli (France), Jacques Mongin knife (France).

These knives are shown larger than actual size.

WHERE COLLECTORS MEET

In the United States, there is at least one knife collectors' fair just about every week-end of the year. Some of the main ones are given below:

• National Knife Collectors' Association fairs. These three-day fairs are held six times a year, in various locations including Louisville, KY; Springfield, MO; and Cincinatti, OH. Contact NKCA, PO Box 21070, Chattanooga, Tennessee TN 37421.

• California Knife Expo, February (3-day).

• Oregon Knife Show, April (2-day).

• Blade Show, Atlanta, May (3-day).

• Custom Knife Show, Orlando, Florida, July (3-day).

In Britain there are no collectors' fairs dedicated exclusively to knives. Knife collectors will, however, find plenty of knives at general militaria fairs, especially the following:

• London Arms Fair. This two-day fair is held twice a year, around the end of April/beginning of May, and the end of September/beginning of October.

• Bedford Arms Fair. A one-day fair held in May and November.

• Birmingham International Arms Fair. One-day fairs held in early March, mid-June, and the end of November at the National Motorcycle Museum.

• Various fairs organized by Sovereign Fairs, Venture House, Fifth Avenue, Letchworth, Herts. SG6 2HW, who also publish *Militaria Collector* magazine (see page 140).

Other fairs are advertised in the magazines listed on page 140. An annual calendar of all UK fairs is available from Central Arms Fairs, 11 Berwick Close, Warwick CV3 5UF.

137

Pierre Calmels in his store at Laguiole (France). Paradise for the devoted enthusiast.

MUSEUMS

In the United States, there are several museums with excellent knife collections on permanent display:

• National Knife Museum, 7201 Shallowford Road, Chattanooga, Tennessee 37421.

• American Military Edged Weaponry Museum, Intercourse, Pennsylvania.

•Knife Museum and Marine Raiders Museum, 1142 W. Grace Street, Richmond, Virginia VA 23220.

There are also extensive knife holdings at the Smithsonian Museum, the Metropolitan Museum of Art in New York, the Oakland Museum in California, the National Metal Museum in Memphis, and a number of others. The knives are not always on permanent display and it is a good idea to check with any museum what their holdings may be.

Much the same is true in Britain, where (for example) Cutlers' Hall in London is not open to the public, though they are willing to show their collection to serious collectors if they make an appointment first. The main public collections are as follows:

• Sheffield City Museum, Weston Park, Sheffield S10.

• Victoria and Albert Museum, Kensington, London.

•The Company of Cutlers in Hallamshire, Cutlers' Hall, Church Street, Sheffield S1.

International travellers will also want to go to Solingen in Germany, where they will find the German Blade Museum and the Solingen Industry Museum. The nearest equivalent in France is the Maison des Couteliers in Thiers.

The town of Laguiole, at the foot of the Aubrac hills in France, and the Calmels knife store. A high point for the traditional French pocket knife.

GUIDE TO FURTHER READING

Collectors in the United States are extremely well served for books on knives. There are rather fewer British books, but both British and American books are available on both sides of the Atlantic.

American Knives, Harold Peterson, Scribners, New York City, 1958.

Encyclopedia of Cutlery Markings, John Goins, Knife World Publications, Knoxville, Tennessee, 1986.

Knives, published annually since 1981; suffixed with date of publication, e.g. "Knives '94." DBI Books, Northbrook, Illinois.

Knives, Points of Interest, Jim Weyer, Weyer International, Toledo, Ohio, 1990 (3 volumes).

Levine's Guide to Knives and Their Values, Bernard Levine, DBI Books, Northbrook, Illinois, 1993 (and periodically updated).

Pen Knives and Other Folding Knives, Simon Moore, Shire Publications, Aylesbury (UK), 1988.

The Standard Knife Collector's Guide, Ron Stewart and Roy Ritchie, Collector Books, Paducah, Kentucky, 1986.

141

If you read French, you would be extremely well advised to get hold of the two books which started it all, *L'Art du Coutelier* (Jean-Jacques Perret, Paris 1771) and *L'Art du Coutelier en Ouvrages Communs* (Fougeroux de Bondaroy, Paris 1771). As for magazines, the leading contenders are mostly American, though the French *La Passion des Couteaux* and the Japanese *Knife* are also excellent.

Blade, Blade Publications, PO Box 22007, Chattanooga, Tennessee TN 37422.

Edges, Blade Publications, PO Box 22007, Chattanooga, Tennessee TN 37422.

National Knife Magazine, PO Box 21070, Chattanooga, Tennessee TN 37421.

Although there are no magazines dedicated specifically to knife collecting in the UK, the collector will find useful information in *Gun Mart*, *Classic Arms and Militaria*, *Militaria Collector*, and *The Armourer*.

Four-piece knife by Jacques Mongin (France) and a Nontron knife (shown closed).

These knives are shown larger than actual size.

Acknowledgments

Special thanks are due to the following, without whose friendly help and advice this book could not have been produced:

Madame Kindal (Coutellerie Kindal), Ms Etsuko Miura (GTI), Monsieur Boissins (Le Couteau de Laguiole), Monsieur Courty (Courty & Fils), Monsieur José Martens (Coutellerie Kindal), Monsieur Gil Szajner (GTI).

Thanks also to the entire team at La Maison de Laguiole in Paris, not forgetting the staff of Établissements Dehillerin and Fred Jouasse.

Sources

All knives illustrated in this book (except where shown as "private collection") were kindly lent by Courty & Fils, Établissements Dehillerin, GTI (fine ceramic blades), Coutellerie Kindal and La Maison de Laguiole.

Technical information comes from the people already mentioned or from the French magazines La Gazette des Couteaux and La Passion des Couteaux (thanks to Yvon Gaguèche!), the American magazine Blade and many of the books shown in the guide to further reading.

Despite every effort we have been unable to trace the exact source of some knives. We extend our apologies to the manufacturers concerned.

Picture credits
All photographs are by Richard Nourry and Matthieu Prier except page 9, top (Hinterleitner/Gamma), pages 13, 14, 15, 136, 138, 139 (Christian Vioujard/Gamma).